THE ETHIOPIAN CRISIS

Touchstone of Appeasement?

PROBLEMS IN EUROPEAN CIVILIZATION

UNDER THE EDITORIAL DIRECTION OF

Ralph W. Greenlaw

Other volumes in preparation

PROBLEMS IN EUROPEAN CIVILIZATION

THE
ETHIOPIAN CRISIS

Touchstone of Appeasement?

EDITED WITH AN INTRODUCTION BY

Ludwig F. Schaefer

CARNEGIE INSTITUTE OF TECHNOLOGY

D. C. HEATH AND COMPANY · BOSTON

Library of Congress Catalog Card number 61-9905

24310

Table of Contents

Introduction

I T is a truism that the proper study of history entails not only the collection of material illuminating certain events but more significantly the understanding of such events. To understand the meaning of the issues with which he is concerned, the student of history must first recapture the characteristic climate of a particular era. This is both his responsibility and his pleasure. The beliefs, the fears and hopes of another generation must become real if he is to evoke an aura of forgotten things. The mark of the great historian is precisely his gift of deep insight into other men and times.

Each age responds, of course, more acutely to some periods of the past than to others. The sixteenth century thus drew its inspiration from classical times, while the early nineteenth century turned often in spirit to the high middle ages. For the present generation, specifically, a certain ambivalence exists toward the kaleidoscopic years preceding the Second World War. On the one hand, one finds easy sympathy for an age which was as truly uncertain as our own. The dilemma of a concentrated attack by alien and foreboding forces upon established values, of democracy faced by a totalitarian system, of inevitable change in a situation where the status quo seemed preferable, is all too familiar. Nor does the mood of millions of peace-loving citizens who sensed the drift of their world toward a catastrophe they could not quite grasp, and felt helpless to prevent, find lack of empathy.

And yet the atmosphere of the nineteen-thirties is strangely disturbing. The very recentness tends to distort. Events within the active memory of man are appraised in the light of consequences then unknown. Here the historian must lift a warning hand. The pre- and post-war worlds are vastly different. The decades between 1914 and 1939 were witness to what now, from the perspective of the Cold War, was clearly the political collapse of Europe.[1] A few perceptive men were aware of this even then. But most clung to their faith that a solution to Europe's difficulties would be found in the re-application of tried and tested formulas which had governed the European political order for centuries. This faith was buttressed by a miscomprehension of the course of recent history and the assurance that the difficulties arose from a temporary disturbance of normal conditions. Observers, made cynical by later experience, are duly critical of the obtuseness and lack of vision of the statesmen of the nineteen-thirties. Yet only by appreciating that they were attempting to meet a challenge within a framework of traditional political attitudes can the student constructively examine the phenomenon of appeasement.

Had it not been for the fact that Ethiopia[2] was a member of the League of Nations — sponsored ironically enough in 1923

[1] Cf. Hajo Holborn, *The Political Collapse of Europe* (New York, 1951), for a masterly development of this argument.

[2] Ethiopia is the official name for the country which is also frequently called Abyssinia (from the Portuguese form of the Arabian "habesch," i.e., mixture). In this booklet both usages have been retained as determined by the authors of the various selections.

by Italy — the crisis which is the subject of the selections in this booklet would no doubt have been little more than a passing squall on the political scene. British and French statesmen, reflecting upon their own colonial history and the exigencies of the political arena, would hardly have gone beyond limited comment on Italian aggression. The abandonment of the backward Ethiopians might even have been turned into a virtue by serving to sate a dissident neighbor. For it was the swelling expression of dissatisfaction with the order which had emerged from Versailles that engendered appeasement. The dictators cleverly oversimplified the distinction between "have" and "have not" nations, but they did accurately reflect a sentiment which had been growing since the peace settlement, that its terms had been unwisely harsh.

To conceive of peace in the strict sense of a state of avoidance of war is meaningless. The existence of peace implies the general acceptance of prevailing political conditions by all or, at least, the significant portion of the community of nations, whereby a modification of these conditions evolves only through orderly and mutually-acceptable means. The political order determined by the provisions of the Treaty of Versailles had been accepted most unwillingly by many nations. That the principal beneficiaries of this arrangement misunderstood the implications of the First World War proved tragic. There were valid reasons why countries such as Italy, Germany, or Japan should desire a readjustment of the system. There were equally sound reasons why the Western democracies would attempt to preserve their own image of the world. But over a decade of involvement with the question of revision had shaken their convictions. Even more telling was the muffled threat of the revisionist states to resort to war if changes were not made.

Weighty moral as well as political and economic considerations lay behind the abhorrence of the democracies for war. When Field Marshal Ludendorff turned to the Fourteen Points in 1918 in his effort to save the German army from destruction, he purportedly declared that Wilson's cant would be the means of entrapping him. In a way, it can be argued that the democracies were indeed "entrapped." Wilsonian aspirations fell ruefully short of post-Versailles reality. Doubt as to its course pervaded the West. "The war to save the world for democracy" proved as much a misnomer as what inexorably would be known as "the war to end war." Disillusion with victory led the democracies to define "peace" narrowly. While they were uncertain of how to entertain a readjustment of the prevalent order, they were determined not to be enticed into further armed conflict. The sanctity of preservation of peace at any price became an article of almost mystic faith. This widespread pacifism, typified by the oath, taken by students at Oxford in 1933, "not to fight for king and country," lies at the root of the practice of appeasement.

A taint of uncleanness has come to cling to the use of this word within the democratic vocabulary. The definition offered in a leading college text of appeasement as "a policy of granting concessions to an aggressive and unscrupulous nation from motives of fear or indolence,"[3] strikes a quicker response than the more restrained explanation in the dictionary, "an act to conciliate." The consequences of appeasement are apparent. The motives of those who turned to appeasement, however, bear closer investigation. The statesmen of the thirties were undeniably foolish to have closed their eyes to the reality of power; they patently accelerated the democratic decline. Is there merit, nonetheless, in exploring the extent to which their parochial interests and indetermination can be distinguished from a conscious surrender of their trust? That they were sheep among wolves — a not unknown species in any historical setting — who sought to redress a critical unbalance by initiating a new era of conciliation? That their crucial mistake lay in a want of unity

[3] Edward McNall Burns and Philip L. Ralph, *World Civilizations* (New York, 1958), 2nd ed., 2 vol., Vol. II, p. 585.

and lack of faith in the principle of collective security, which had become the backbone of the post-war order?

Reflections of this sort explain why the selections which follow focus upon the activity surrounding the consideration of the Ethiopian issue by the League of Nations. It is, indeed, the peculiar involvement of the League, quite distinct from its procedure in other crises, which raises the question, lying at the heart of this collection of commentary, whether the Italian-Ethiopian conflict was not the very touchstone of appeasement. The principle of collective security as an instrument for securing the peace was the victim of prenatal malnutrition. Abandoned by its natural parent at birth, nursed by indifferent guardians, it succumbed in early adolescence. The League proved able to impose its will only in quarrels concerning minor powers. With the absence of the United States and the Soviet Union and the disinterest of Great Britain, France made use of the League structure to enhance her own security position. The British, in their turn, misconstrued French fear of Germany as a renewal of her ancient ambition to dominate Europe. The resulting joust kept the democracies at cross purposes and made it relatively easy for Japan to carry out in 1931 her aggressive policy in Manchuria. The League, to be sure, investigated and declared its disapproval. The United States concurred. But French attention was fixed on Europe; Britain and America could not decide whether to act — either independently or in unison — in preservation of their special interests in the Pacific. For those with eyes to see, Manchuria hinted at the moral bankruptcy of League leadership. And yet the crisis which arose out of the Wal Wal incident provides an even more instructive example of collective security under attack. In 1935–36, amidst a great paeon of sonorous righteousness, the League mobilized its machinery and displayed its impotence to the world. The readings in this volume should allow the student to determine to what degree the ramifications of the Italian-Ethiopian imbroglio may serve as a microcosm of the dilemma of the nineteen-thirties.

Professor Toynbee, in fact, in the second selection, sees it as the tragedy of Western society in which the Mussolinian sin of commission had combined with the democratic sin of omission to expose "the moral perversity" of the Christian world. That being so, Western man must share the ultimate guilt for the destruction of his own heritage and the transfer of power to totalitarianism. G. M. Gathorne-Hardy recognizes the justice of this judgment in essence if not in form. He devotes a lengthy chapter in his survey of international events between the wars to the Ethiopian crisis because it is to him a crucial turning-point in post-war history which affected the whole world with fundamental consequences.

Winston Churchill was one of the very few European statesmen who were alive to the portents of the times. The menace of an unleashed Nazi Germany was unmistakable to him. A Conservative, with all the understandable reluctance of his class to jeopardize further a social and economic status which participation in the First World War had badly weakened, Churchill, no less than his fellows, desired to avoid a conflict with Italy. Whereas their attitude, however, was rooted in a general averseness toward any action which might entail British energy and expense, his grew from the fear of driving Mussolini into the camp of Hitler. In spite of a practical desire to accommodate Italy where possible, Churchill saw plainly what most of his fellow Conservatives did not: that Italy, having scorned a reasonable solution to her aspirations, must be clearly and decisively curbed lest the West bare its weakness to other aggressors.

Whether, had Churchill been in a position to exert leadership, the Italian-Ethiopian crisis would have been of short duration and the dictators firmly tethered can only be surmised. It is the conviction of Professor Salvemini in the fourth selection that absence of British resistance to Italian pretensions — he suggests a certain alacrity to agree to a sharing of colonial spoils — was directly responsible for World War II. Another Italian historian, Luigi Villari, argues quite the opposite in coming to a similar conclusion. British jealousy in sharing Africa and a calculated attempt to make political hay in the parliamentary elections of Fall, 1935, by blackening the name of Italy provide him ground for branding "Edenism" as the cause for subsequent disasters.

Others have placed the primary guilt with France. Terrified by the sight of a resurgent Germany, she sought to broaden her ring of alliances. Ethiopia was the price of Italian cooperation with France. Lord Vansittart, Permanent Under-Secretary in the British Foreign Office between 1930 and 1938, claims that Premier Pierre Laval was in the pay of both Mussolini and Hitler,[4] but Vansittart in his anxiety to prevent a merging of German and Italian interests was involved in the fiasco of the Hoare-Laval Plan and was understandably bitter at its premature release by the French. It is probably safe to assume that all Frenchmen — including the slippery and self-seeking Laval — who were not completely obsessed with the Red bogey were hostile to a rampant Germany. They were, however, by no means united in playing fast with the existing deterrent to renewed German expansion, the League of Nations, in order to gain the support of Mussolini. It is interesting to speculate whether the French plan of augmenting their position was ever possible. Could a nation which was vitally interested in preserving the status quo come to terms with one whose ideology had as a prime tenet the increase of its power? Or was it the sudden-found British championship of the League which distorted an otherwise workable scheme and promoted a wave of double-dealing all along the line from Mussolini to Laval to Baldwin to Hitler? This is the topic of concern for

Arnold Wolfers and D. W. Brogan in the sixth and seventh selections.

But, as Sigmund Neumann indicates, it is difficult and quite misleading to separate French and British failings. The Ethiopian crisis became a "test of political astuteness and moral fiber of the great powers." Mussolini was eager to utilize the menace of Hitler and the need for a united front to add to his empire. France was prepared to walk a precarious diplomatic tightrope to procure an illusive security. Soviet Russia donned ill-fitting democratic garb in alarm over the implications of continued isolation. And Britain, preferring the comforting blindness of the ostrich, gave lip service to her illustrious heritage.

All would agree, however, that the victor was Adolf Hitler. The net result of Ethiopia was the formation of the Rome-Berlin Axis in which Mussolini emerged as the junior partner of the German Fuehrer. Could this fatal denouement have been avoided? Elizabeth Wiskemann concludes that a careful handling of the crisis could have prevented an alliance, the impetus for which originated with Hitler and not with Mussolini. The character of the two dictators was generally misassessed at the time. Mussolini's bluster was weighed more heavily than the facts merited. The impact of Hitler's demonic intensity was still not apparent. With his usual prescience he saw in Ethiopian developments the opportunity to bind Italy to his dream of German world hegemony. The association did not accord with Italy's natural interests, but the irresolute actions of the democracies forfeited for them the power of leverage which had been the dominant feature of their control of Europe. Hitler reaped the harvest which grew from the confusion in which Britain and France found themselves when faced simultaneously with two revisionist attacks. Alan Bullock points out the superior realism of Hitler and his brilliant exploitation of the unexpected moment in the tenth selection.

There are those who would still maintain that the Ethiopian crisis was primarily one more case of European power politics. Her-

---

[4] Robert Vansittart, *Lessons of My Life* (New York, 1943), pp. 37–52.

bert Feis is concerned with its reverberations in the United States and the vital importance of the American attitude. Since League leadership was shaky at best, the position of the United States became a material consideration. Sanctions could not be effective without the concurrence of the United States. But American public opinion held that the country, having burned her fingers once, should avoid foreign entanglements. The spate of neutrality legislation was enacted just at the time when continental statesmen were nervously considering what the consequences might be if full-blown sanctions, as many believed, would drive Mussolini to war. The possibility that American neutrality might actually work in favor of Mussolini against the democracies dampened, Feis sadly concludes, their spirit of resistance.

Once again the American reaction was not unique but contributed to a current which flowed over the whole Western world. Peace meant the avoidance of war. Each nation held to its own ivory tower, be that the barrier of a broad ocean, a readiness not to let one hand see what the other was doing or a blind trust in the panacea of collective security. The indictment by Richard Crossman, which stands at the end of this booklet, of Western abandonment of intrinsic values and of passive reliance on right-sounding sentiment without the will to translate words into action recalls the anguished cry of Alexis de Tocqueville to the French Chamber of Deputies just before the February Revolution that it was the spirit and not the laws which really counted. May not the Italian-Ethiopian crisis, wrapped in its mantle of appeasement, be the source of fruitful inquiry into an ageless problem?

LIST OF IMPORTANT EVENTS

1933 January 30   Hitler becomes German Chancellor
June 7   Four-Power Pact
October 14   German withdrawal from Disarmament Conference and League

1934 January 26   German-Polish Non-Aggression Pact
June 30   Blood Purge in Germany
July 26   Austrian Putsch
September 18   Russia joins the League of Nations
October 13   Assassination of Barthou and King Alexander in Marseilles; Laval French Foreign Minister
November 12   Vote on Peace Ballot begins
December 5   Wal Wal Incident (Ual Ual)

1935 January 4–7   Laval-Mussolini negotiations in Rome
January 13   Saar Plebiscite
March 16   Reintroduction of German conscription
April 11–14   Stresa Conference
May 2   Franco-Soviet Pact of Mutual Assistance
June 18   Anglo-German Naval Accord
June 24–26   Eden visit to Rome to negotiate the Ethiopian dispute
June 27   Announcement of Peace Ballot results
August 31   American Neutrality Resolution
September 11   Speech of Sir Samuel Hoare to League
October 3   Italy invades Ethiopia
October 10   League Committee on Sanctions
November 14   British General Elections
December 9   Hoare-Laval Plan

1936 March 7   German reoccupation of the Rhineland
May 5   Italian Forces enter Addis Ababa
July 4   League Council votes to discontinue Sanctions
July 18   Outbreak of Spanish Civil War
October 26   Rome-Berlin Axis

The Conflict of Opinion

"[The Abyssinian crisis] marks a crucial turning-point in post-war history. The triumph of Italian aggression, naked and unashamed, affected the whole world with fundamental consequences. To England, it meant the virtual destruction of the institution which successive Governments, of different parties, had proclaimed to be the keystone of their foreign policy. To France . . . it meant that the enemy of whom she stood most in terror was encouraged to fresh audacity and rescued from his previous isolation. And finally, by an act of poetic justice, it was destined to mean the extinction of [Italy's] influence on the Danube, and the arrival of German forces on the Brenner."

— G. M. Gathorne-Hardy

"A spirit of collective pacifism possessed them, and made the peoples content with the lazy approval of high ideals, the verbal condemnation of injustice, chicanery and oppression. . . . It intoxicated the democracies with a feeling of moral superiority and well-being, while it sapped their sense of responsibility. Gradually statesmen and peoples alike began to believe that the League of Nations was a force able to do the work which previously fell to the various nations. . . . Since the League had no coercive power at its disposal, this trust was wholly unjustified."

— R. H. S. Crossman

"The Italo-Ethiopian War marked a milestone in the evolution of public opinion, which often proved to be more sincere and more advanced in realizing the issues, dangers, and necessary decisions than were the statesmen."

— Sigmund Neumann

"History has perhaps never played a stranger trick upon Man than to allow British indignation against international lawlessness and imperialist and racial bullying to have smoothed the path of Adolf Hitler. Out of this misconception was born that deformity, the Italo-German alliance, of which Hitler had so long dreamed."

— Elizabeth Wiskemann

"The policy of appeasement is not to be understood unless it is realized that it represented the acceptance by the British Government, at least in part, of Hitler's view of what British policy should be."

— Alan Bullock

"If ever there was an opportunity of striking a decisive blow in a generous cause with a minimum of risk, it was here and now. The fact that the nerve of the British Government was not equal to the occasion can be excused only by their sincere love of peace."

— WINSTON CHURCHILL

"But for Eden's blocking of peace moves before 1939, it is likely that there would have been no war in 1939. . . . In short, Edenism from 1934 to 1938 was responsible for Churchill and the disastrous impact of the latter's policies on Britain, Europe and the world."

— LUIGI VILLARI

". . . it is apparent that the sin which was committed in 1935 was not merely Mussolini's or Fascismo's or Italy's. This guilt was shared by Britain and France, and in some measure by the whole living generation of the Western Society."

— ARNOLD TOYNBEE

"There was only one country strong enough and free enough to turn the balance of events against [Mussolini], if it so willed — the United States."

— HERBERT FEIS

ITALY AND ABYSSINIA

G. M. GATHORNE-HARDY

Geoffrey Malcolm Gathorne-Hardy served with distinction in the Boer and First World Wars and was thereafter long-time honorary secretary of the Royal Institute of International Affairs. It was to complement the annual survey of international affairs directed by Professor Arnold Toynbee and to reach some kind of retrospect over the happenings of the years since the war that *A Short History of International Affairs* appeared in 1934. The following selection, drawn from the Fourth Edition (1950), serves as a general introduction to the events of the year 1935.

THE FRANCO-ITALIAN AGREEMENTS

THE first event of international importance in the year 1935 was an endeavour on the part of France to consolidate her newly won friendship with Italy. During practically the whole of the post-war period down to July 1934, a variety of causes had subjected Franco-Italian relations to considerable tension, and the policy of Italy had been on the whole extremely sympathetic to Germany. M. Barthou had been succeeded as French Foreign Minister by a man whose character and personality were destined to exert so decisive an influence on the events recorded in this chapter that he merits a few words of introduction. M. Pierre Laval, the individual in question, has been pungently described by Lord Vansittart, who had first-rate opportunities of studying him at close quarters, as — in the category of "rotters" — "one of the few in whom the microscope has revealed nothing but more teeming decomposition." Nature, in casting him for the role of a crook and a traitor, seemed to have overdone the make-up. In spite, however, of a reptilian countenance calculated to inspire the liveliest mistrust, M. Laval succeeded, over a number of years,

in playing the part most competently. Lord Vansittart suggests that as early as 1935 he was already prepared to betray his country's interests both to Hitler and Mussolini. But it is proposed here to give him the benefit of the doubt, and to interpret his actions on the hypothesis that his aims at this stage may have been those of a patriotic but narrow-minded Frenchman, though the means by which he sought to achieve them were completely unscrupulous and dishonest. M. Laval lost no time in attempting to exploit the favourable circumstances which had brought about the reorientation of so important a European Power. Immediately after the New Year he set out for Rome, where, in the course of three days, agreement was reached on a number of outstanding questions. A concession of further territory in Africa, considerable in extent though of small value, was made by France to Italy in supplementary and final redemption of her pledge in the Treaty of London, 1915. Further compensations to Italy in Africa took the form of an arrangement for a transfer of some 2,500 shares in the French-owned Djibouti-Addis Ababa railway, through which the trade of Abyssinia was connected with the sea in French Somaliland. On

From G. M. Gathorne-Hardy, *A Short History of International Affairs 1920–1939* (London, 1950), pp. 392–418. Published under the auspices of the Royal Institute of International Affairs. Reprinted by permission of Oxford University Press.

1

the Tunisian issue, a settlement was arrived at whereby children born of Italian parents in that colony before 1945 should retain Italian nationality, and those born in the ensuing twenty years should have a right of option. After 1965 the French common law was to prevail.

In reference to the European situation, both parties agreed to act in concert in the event of a unilateral repudiation by any country of its armaments obligations, and recognized the principle that no such unilateral action was permissible. They reaffirmed the obligation to respect the independence and territorial integrity of other States, and recommended the conclusion of a convention for reciprocal non-intervention between Austria and other "particularly interested States." Superficially, it appeared that Italy had derived few advantages from this bargain. The willingness of France to co-operate in opposition to German interference with Austria seemed a foregone conclusion in any case, for which no payment was required; the Tunisian arrangements involved on the whole a relaxation of the claims previously made by Italy, and the territorial gains in Africa amounted to no more than a number of square miles of thinly populated desert. Having regard to the sequel, there can be little doubt that the aspect of the Franco-Italian settlement to which Signor Mussolini attached the greatest importance was that it would clear the way for a project, plans for which had been for some time in preparation — the conquest of Abyssinia. Hitherto, an Italian forward policy in this region would have been met by the jealous opposition of France, but, at the present juncture, as the very fact of the negotiations tended to prove, the situation arising from the resurgence of Germany made her inclined to subordinate all other interests to the paramount aim of organizing a common front against the European peril. In the Rome conversations Signor Mussolini obtained at least an assurance that the direct interests of France would not stand in the way of the establishment by Italy of a predominant economic influence in Abyssinia, and, though M. Laval was perhaps truthful in asserting that "nothing in the Rome Agreements tampers with the sovereignty, independence, and territorial integrity of Ethiopia," and in repudiating the charge that he had given *carte blanche* in advance to Italian aggression, the Duce appears to have concluded, rightly in the light of what followed, that if French interests were no bar to his plans, Ethiopian interests were not a matter in which France would be greatly concerned.

THE FIRST REPUDIATION OF THE VERSAILLES TREATY

Meanwhile, Herr Hitler was realizing the advisability of some sensational stroke of policy to vindicate his claim to be the destined leader to bring his nation from the Egyptian bondage of the Peace Treaty into the Promised Land of German hegemony. Progress had so far been slow and unimpressive. The Anschluss seemed farther off than ever, and the main result of the Austrian *putsch* had been to turn a probable ally into an active opponent. It was true that the work of rearming Germany had already surreptitiously begun, but it seemed probable that it might be robbed of dramatic interest by the acquiescence of the other Powers, so long as it was not too defiantly advertised. From the conversations between France and Great Britain which took place in London at the beginning of February 1935, it was apparent that both Governments were prepared, conditionally, to abrogate the disarmament clauses of Versailles. The condition which France was most anxious to impose was the adherence of Germany to the system of mutual guarantee projected by M. Barthou, and this idea found expression in the communiqué issued at the conclusion of the London conversations, where it was coupled with a new proposal for an "air Locarno," under which the Western Powers would mutually undertake to give the immediate assistance of their air forces to whichever of them might be the victim of unprovoked aerial aggression by another of the contracting parties.

These proposals were presented to Germany as an integral whole, since the point on which British opinion was most insistent was the attainment of a general settlement; in Germany, however, they were considered separately and met with different receptions. The air-pact, which, as General Göring later pointed out, implied the existence of the air force denied by the Peace Treaty to Germany, was decidedly welcomed; to refuse such a proposal would merely be to deprive Germany of the contingent benefits of an arrangement which the other parties were quite capable of concluding between themselves, but Germany maintained her objections to entering into multilateral pacts in eastern Europe. Still, the prospects seemed sufficiently favourable to warrant an invitation to Sir John Simon to visit Berlin on 7 March. Three days, however, before the date proposed, the British Government published a parliamentary paper relating to the question of defence. This drew attention to the "fact that Germany was . . . rearming openly on a large scale, despite the provisions of Part V of the Treaty of Versailles," and recognized "that not only the forces but the spirit in which the population, and especially the youth of the country, are being organized lend colour to, and substantiate, the general feeling of insecurity which has already been incontestably generated."

Whether in consequence of this outspoken publication, as was generally assumed at the time, or from other causes, Herr Hitler immediately developed "a cold," which necessitated the postponement of the British visit until towards the end of the month. His recovery from this diplomatic ailment was further jeopardized by a decision of the French Cabinet, on 12 March, to make up the serious deficiency in available conscripts which faced them during the years 1935–9, owing to the fall in the French birth-rate during the Great War. This end they proposed to attain by doubling the period of service and reducing the age of enlistment. Though this would not result in an expansion of the French forces, but was merely designed to maintain them at the normal level of about 350,000 men, it supplied the Führer with a convenient pretext for a step which he may already have contemplated. It was by this time evident that the policy both of France and Great Britain contemplated, as inevitable, an increase in the armed forces of Germany; it was therefore a safe conjecture that neither of them would proceed to extremities, however flagrantly Herr Hitler chose to repudiate his obligations under Part V of the Peace Treaty. In these circumstances, he was presented with the opportunity for a dramatic *coup*.

On Saturday, 9 March, foreign Governments were officially notified of the existence, in spite of the Treaty, of a German air force. This date is of importance as marking the first open repudiation by Germany of her treaty obligations, but the essential fact had for some time been common property, and the announcement, therefore, while it may have been intended as a *ballon d'essai*, fell comparatively flat. On the 13th Sir John Simon stated, in the House of Commons, that the postponed Anglo-German discussions would take place on the 25th, and that he and Mr. Eden would leave for Berlin on the previous day. The next week-end was, however, more sensational. On 16 March the Government of the Reich published a decree reintroducing conscription in Germany, and placing the peace-strength of the German army at twelve corps and thirty-six divisions, or, as Herr Hitler subsequently paraphrased it, about 550,000 men. As a force of this size nearly doubled the figure which Herr Hitler had previously proposed as adequate, and was overwhelmingly in excess of the normal peace-strength of the French army in Europe, the announcement aroused general consternation. As the British Government hastened to point out in an official protest, it gravely impaired, if it did not finally destroy, the prospects of a "general settlement freely negotiated," which had hitherto been the accepted objective of European diplomacy:

The attainment of a comprehensive agreement, which by common consent would take the place of treaty provisions, cannot be facilitated by putting forward, as a decision already arrived at, strengths for military effectives greatly exceeding any before suggested — strengths, moreover, which, if maintained unaltered, must make more difficult, if not impossible, the agreement of other Powers vitally concerned.

The French and Italian Governments also protested, and the former lodged an immediate appeal with the Secretary General of the League. An extraordinary meeting of the League Council was summoned, to be preceded by a conference between the representatives of France, Great Britain, and Italy, at Stresa, on 11 April, to consider the attitude of these three Powers to the new situation.

THE STRESA CONFERENCE AND THE PROCEEDINGS AT GENEVA.

The visit of the British Ministers to Berlin took place, as arranged, on 25 March, but achieved little more than the disclosure of a stubborn and recalcitrant attitude on the part of Herr Hitler. It was followed by the visit of Mr. Eden to Moscow, Warsaw, and Prague, and by the meeting of the Stresa Conference on 11 April. This was mainly an attempt to demonstrate a common front. The three Governments

regretfully recognized that the method of unilateral repudiation adopted by the German Government, at a moment when steps were being taken to promote a freely negotiated settlement of the question of armaments, had undermined public confidence in the security of a peaceful order.

They reaffirmed their loyalty to the Locarno Treaty, and, recurring to the subject of Austria,

confirmed the Anglo-Franco-Italian declarations of the 17th February and the 27th

September, 1934, in which the three Governments recognized that the necessity of maintaining the independence and integrity of Austria would continue to inspire their common policy.

It was, perhaps, significant that Signor Mussolini issued on the morning of the Conference a warning to the Italian people not to expect too much from its deliberations. At this time his mind was already occupied with a project subversive of peace and fatal to collaboration, to which, by a conspiracy of silence, no allusion was made at the Conference by any of the parties.

The subsequent proceedings of the Council of the League, which deliberated at Geneva from 15-17 April, resulted in a declaration that:

Germany has failed in the obligation which lies upon all the members of the international community to respect the undertaking which they have contracted,

and in a hint that verbal reproof might be supplemented by positive action, if any further actions of the kind condemned were to take place.

In this connexion it was decided that repudiation of the kind of which Germany had been judged guilty should, "in the event of its having relation to undertakings concerning the security of peoples and the maintenance of peace *in Europe*," call into play appropriate measures, and a committee was requested

to propose for this purpose measures to render the Covenant more effective in the organization of collective security, and to define in particular the economic and financial measures which might be applied should, in the future, a State, whether a member of the League of Nations or not, endanger peace by the unilateral repudiation of its international obligations.

The rather strange limitation to "the security of people and the maintenance of peace *in Europe*" attracted some attention at the time, and more later. It was evidently deliberate, for an attempt by M. Litvinov to widen the scope of the resolution was keenly resisted, but it might be justified in that the aim was to devise a new sanction for something not expressly dealt with in the Covenant, and that in instituting fresh punitive legislation it was advisable not to propose anything which might not command general approval. It seems clearly mistaken to read into the words a hidden reference to the Abyssinian situation, which, if it resulted in aggression, was already covered by Article 16.

HERR HITLER'S SPEECH OF 21 MAY 1935

Those who adopted the more favourable view of Herr Hitler's intentions and policy could at this stage cite in support of their thesis the reasonableness and moderation of his attitude as expressed in an important speech which he delivered on 21 May. It is important, in view of subsequent developments, to remember that this exhaustive and deliberate pronouncement on German foreign policy was uttered immediately after the signature of the French and Czechoslovak pacts with the Soviet Union, which, indeed, it treated as a factor in the situation, since it stated that:

as a result of *the military alliance between France and Russia,* an element of legal insecurity has been brought into the Locarno Pact,

and accordingly —

the German Government would be specially grateful for an authentic interpretation of the retrospective and future effects of *the Franco-Russian military alliance* on the contractual obligations of the single parties who signed the Locarno Pact.

It was therefore with a full recognition of this treaty as a *fait accompli* that Herr Hitler, while justifying his unilateral repudiation of the imposed Treaty of Versailles, especially since, on his interpretation, the understanding as to disarmament had been previously broken by the other parties, gave

an assurance that he would faithfully observe international obligations voluntarily assumed, and in particular the Locarno Treaty, including its provisions with regard to the demilitarized zone in the Rhineland. On this subject he spoke as follows:

In particular they (the German Government) will uphold and fulfil all obligations arising out of the Locarno Treaty so long as the other partners on their side are ready to stand by that pact. In respecting the demilitarized zone the German Government consider their action as a contribution to the appeasement of Europe, which contribution is of an unheard-of hardness for a sovereign State.

While this sentence may possibly now be interpreted as concealing a means of escape from the policy which it proclaimed, it can hardly be regarded as an honest indication that the pledge could not, in fact, be relied on.

Even more specific was the declaration made in the same speech with regard to Austria:

Germany neither intends nor wishes to interfere in the internal affairs of Austria, to annex Austria, or to conclude an Anschluss.

With regard to the rearmament of Germany, Herr Hitler was equally modest and reassuring. He would in no circumstances depart from the scale announced, and was ready at any time to limit the forces of Germany to any extent equally adopted by the other Powers. In the air, he claimed no more than parity with the Western European nations, and at sea he was willing to limit the German navy to 35 per cent of the British, and disclaimed any intention to approach naval rearmament in a competitive spirit. Finally, he protested against "irresponsible propaganda," and urged the desirability of an international agreement to exclude external interference with the domestic affairs of any nation.

Strangely as some passages in this speech may read in the light of subsequent events, it produced at the time a satisfactory impression of pacific intentions and not unreasonable demands. Those, however, who doubted the sincerity of the speaker could point out that some reassurance to the troubled mind of Europe was urgently called for in the circumstances. The *fait accompli* of 16 March had resulted in a defensive consolidation of all the remaining Great Powers of Europe, for to the three participants at Stresa the Franco-Russian treaty had now linked the Soviet Union. In addition to this the League of Nations had been induced seriously to consider the planning of effective steps to prevent the repetition of such a *coup*. Nothing further could be gained by truculence, and existing gains might be expected in these conditions to resort to fair words and specious promises, to lull the suspicions which had been aroused, while losing no opportunity of attempting to sow dissension in the ranks now arrayed against him. Proposals such as the Führer now put forward were calculated to bring into conflict the sceptical legalism of France and the British predilection for compromise; the widespread unpopularity of the Franco-Soviet Pact was a source of discord which might be profitably exploited, but the distinction drawn between armament by sea and land was also a promising instrument to serve the same purpose.

THE ANGLO-GERMAN NAVAL AGREEMENT

The sincerity of Herr Hitler's offer in regard to naval armament seemed less open to question than that of any other part of his proposals. In *Mein Kampf* he shows a clear perception of the folly of following a "Drang nach Osten" with an antagonized England in the rear:

Only with England was it possible, with the rear protected, to begin the new German advance. . . . No sacrifice should have been too great to win England's favour.

Among the necessary sacrifices enumerated in the above passage he included the "re-nunciation of a German navy." Later on, with the revival of designs upon a colonial empire, this programme might be revised, but, so long as the objectives were expansion in the east and the destruction of French hegemony, Herr Hitler would be ready enough to reassure the misgivings of the predominant maritime Power. The British Government was therefore quite justified in believing that the naval part of the German offer was genuine and trustworthy.

True to the British spirit of compromise, they hastened to make sure of the half loaf obtainable. On 4 June negotiations were begun, and on the 18th an agreement was completed. The ratio of 35:100 which had been offered by Herr Hitler was adhered to in this document, though Germany also acquired the right to a submarine tonnage equal to the total in this category possessed by the entire British Commonwealth, so long as the arrangement as to total tonnage was not transgressed. There is no doubt that naval construction at least up to these limits would in any case have been undertaken, and had, indeed, already begun. As far back as 26 April the German Government had announced to Great Britain the construction of a number of submarines, in clear contravention of Article 191 of the Peace Treaty. As early as 8 July a German naval building programme was published, comprising two 26,000-ton battleships, two 10,000-ton cruisers, sixteen destroyers of 1,625 tons each, and twenty submarines, and there is good reason to believe that some progress had been made with this programme before 18 June. Considered in isolation, from the British point of view, there was everything to be said for the policy of imposing, while the opportunity was open, some agreed limit upon the naval rearmament of Germany. If the agreement had been concluded in collaboration with France and Italy, it would have been unobjectionable.

None the less, what was done amounted to a condonation by Great Britain alone of a further breach of a treaty obligation. By

England's action, the common diplomatic front agreed on at Stresa had been broken. Equally, what was done was a departure from the standpoint agreed on by France and Great Britain in February, that German release from the restrictions of Versailles should only be conceded as part of a general settlement. France and Italy showed clear signs of dissatisfaction. England appeared in their eyes too readily to have swallowed a bait artfully dangled before her by the German dictator. If the primary purpose of Herr Hitler's offer had been to shake the solidarity of the "Stresa Front," it had certainly achieved its object.

THE ITALO-ABYSSINIAN WAR

This solidarity was, however, much more seriously threatened by the Italian determination to engage in war with Abyssinia, which was by this time beginning to be generally apprehended. It is now known, thanks to the candid disclosures of Marshal Emilio de Bono, that this determination had been irrevocably formed at least as far back as the autumn of 1933, and that from this point forward Italy had been working energetically, against time, to prepare for war by a date which would allow the affair to be settled no later than 1936. Much had to be done in a short time, but by entrusting the preparations and the command in the coming campaign to de Bono, a man already 67 years of age in 1933, the Duce ensured that everything possible would be done to avoid postponement of the date arranged. A year or two later the General would be too old to realize his cherished ambition of ending his military career with a high command on active service. It was originally contemplated that this planned act of aggression should be camouflaged either as intervention in an internal rebellion in Abyssinia, or what the Marshal suggestively calls a "manoeuvred defence followed by a counter-offensive." Energetic efforts were therefore made from the first to subvert, by intrigue and bribery, the loyalty of the subordinate Ethiopian chiefs, a policy which, though it never got so far

as to supply a pretext for intervention, proved of considerable value in the subsequent campaign.

The important thing to understand is this: that from the very outset of the campaign there were signs of the results of this disintegrating political action, and that it deprived our enemy of at least 200,000 men.

The alternative pretext broke down through the refusal of the victim to be provoked into offensive action, and his disconcerting readiness to afford satisfaction for any "incidents." Hence, when the prearranged moment arrived, all attempts at disguise had to be abandoned.

From the plan of a maneuvred defensive followed by a counter-offensive we were obliged to change over to the plan of an offensive action.

The grounds of the Duce's decision, taken in 1933, immediately after the accession of Herr Hitler to power in Germany, may be assumed to have been approximately the following. Italy's need for expansion was a fundamental postulate of Fascist policy. Asia Minor having been ruled out, first by the Peace Conference and finally by the resurgence of Turkey, there remained two alternative possibilities — "pacific expansion towards the east," converting the whole Danubian and Balkan region so far as possible into an Italian protectorate or sphere of influence, or the acquisition of increased colonial territory in Africa. In this region, however, whatever may have been Signor Mussolini's ultimate dreams of Mediterranean hegemony, there was only one piece of territory the acquisition of which did not involve direct collision with a rival European Power. This was the Empire of Ethiopia, a region where the temptation to a forward policy was peculiarly strong, firstly, because of its potential wealth and resources, but also because, by the Treaty of Ucciali in 1889, the Italians had once before believed themselves to have acquired a protectorate over it, until the denunciation of the treaty by Menelik in 1893, and the disastrous defeat at Adowa in 1896, temporarily destroyed these hopes, and left only a rankling and vindictive memory. But, although the other European Powers concerned, Great Britain and France, had long recognized a wide sphere of Italian interest in the Ethiopian Empire, until the European situation was modified by the arrival of Herr Hitler any further possibilities of colonial expansion here, as elsewhere in Africa, were liable to meet with the opposition of France, if not of England. Both these Powers, together with Italy, were in fact bound by the Tripartite Agreement of 1906 to make every effort to preserve the integrity of Ethiopia. French opposition had therefore hitherto barred the complete realization of either of the alternative schemes for Italian expansion; in south-east Europe, through the relations of France with the Little Entente, and in Africa, because of competing French interests in all of the coveted regions. In the event of Germany, under the new dispensation, growing strong enough to pursue the declared plans of the Führer, Italian predominance on the Danube was equally barred, but these plans were at least equally prejudicial to French interests, and it might in these circumstances be possible to play upon the European fears of France sufficiently to disinterest her in the fate of Abyssinia. Having regard to the European situation, and the attitude hitherto adopted by the League towards extra-European wars (e.g. the Manchurian affair and the struggle between Bolivia and Paraguay), the project of aggression against Abyssinia seemed to be a relatively safe speculation.

It was true that, in the earlier post-war years, an endeavour had been made to establish Italian influence in Abyssinia by peaceful and co-operative methods; it was largely on the Italian recommendation that Abyssinia had been admitted to membership of the League in 1923, against the inclination of Great Britain; but the use which Abyssinia had made of her new status was not encouraging from the Italian standpoint, since an attempt in 1925 by Italy and Great Britain to apportion Abyssinian spheres of influence without consulting the third party affected had been met, and partially frustrated, by an Ethiopian appeal to the League. In 1928 a final effort to secure Italian interests by peaceful means took the form of an Italo-Abyssinian treaty, by which, *inter alia*, the parties pledged themselves not to take action detrimental to the independence of each other, and to submit all disputes to conciliation and arbitration, without resorting to armed force.

With the rise of the Nazi menace, however, it now appeared safe to pursue Italian ends by more vigorous and far-reaching action.

Though the unruliness of the border tribes had undoubtedly given constant trouble to all Abyssinia's neighbours, none of them had hitherto thought of making these periodical acts of irresponsible banditry an excuse for punitive action against the Empire, whose ruler, Ras Tafari, who succeeded as Haile Selassie I in November 1930, was an Ethiopian of exceptional enlightenment, and animated by a sincere spirit of reform. The first warning of serious trouble impending between Italy and Abyssinia occurred on 5 September 1934, when a clash occurred between some Italian and Abyssinian forces in the neighbourhood of Walwal, as a result of which 30 Italian native soldiers were killed and 100 wounded, while the casualties on the other side were considerably heavier. Having regard to what is now known of the Italian intentions, and to the fact that the subsequent decision of the Conciliation Commission (on 3 September 1935) exonerated both sides, the merits of the Walwal dispute are now a matter of minor importance. The Italians consistently refused to allow the discussion of the preliminary question — whether the attack took place in Italian or Abyssinian territory; though the frontier was undefined, there is a strong case for deciding that Walwal lay some sixty miles within the Ethiopian border.

The area had, however, been under Italian control, not officially recognized by the Abyssinians, since 1928, and permanently occupied since 1930. It is impossible to be certain which side fired the first shot.

The Walwal incident was, however, the occasion whereby the Italo-Abyssinian crisis first came within the purview of the League. On 14 December the Italian Government had refused a proposal by the Abyssinians to refer the dispute to arbitration under the treaty of 1928, on the ground that the facts were indisputable, and on the same day the Ethiopian Government accordingly telegraphed to the Secretary-General of the League, informing him of the situation and alleging further Italian acts of aggression. But it was not until 3 January 1935, that they lodged a formal appeal to Article II of the Covenant.

From the point of view of the European Powers, and especially of France, this development could hardly have taken place at a more inconvenient moment. It practically synchronized with the visit of M. Laval to Rome, in an attempt to effect a close and durable *rapprochement* with Italy. In these circumstances, the Italian Government was persuaded to accept the suggestion of settling the incident by arbitration under the 1928 treaty, and the appeal was consequently withdrawn from the League agenda. In the following month, however, the military preparations of Italy were so formidably apparent that from this date little doubt remained, in the mind of anyone not troubled by diplomatic considerations, as to her aggressive intentions. At the same time, the proposed arbitral proceedings were brought to deadlock by a fundamental divergence as to the scope of the inquiry, and on 17 March the Abyssinian Government formally appealed to the League under Article 15.

This date was once more a peculiarly unfortunate one, since it coincided exactly with Herr Hitler's unilateral repudiation of the disarmament provisions of Versailles. Though, as early as February, the British Ambassador in Rome had warned Signor Mussolini "of the possible reactions of Italian policy on British public opinion and on Anglo-Italian relations," it appeared at this stage regrettably tactless to hint that the promising new recruit to the police force enrolled for the control of Germany was contemplating an independent act of gangsterism of his own. The League accordingly welcomed the leisurely and obstructed progress of the negotiations for settlement, in spite of protests from the Ethiopians that these delays were merely facilitating the perfection of Italian military preparations. The Stresa Conference drew further attention to the importance of consolidating the anti-German front, and the Council, in its ensuing extraordinary session, postponed consideration of the Italo-Abyssinian dispute till the following month. On 25 May the Council left the settlement of the dispute still in the hands of the two parties, with the proviso that it would meet again to consider the matter if the final arbitrator had not been selected by 25 July, or if the settlement had not been concluded by the same day of the following month.

The first contingency was duly brought about by the breakdown of the Commission on 9 July, but in the meantime the British Government had made an independent effort at mediation. On a visit to Rome in the latter part of June, Mr. Eden suggested to the Duce the cession to Italy by Abyssinia of a portion of the Ogaden, in return for an outlet to the sea at Zeila in British Somaliland. In reporting his refusal to entertain this proposal to Marshal de Bono, Signor Mussolini wrote: "You can imagine my reply. . . . The English attitude has helped instead of injuring. . . . You have then only 120 days in which to get ready." "Actually," records the Marshal, "I had less."

The extraordinary meeting of the Council occasioned by the breakdown of the Commission took place on 31 July. It now succeeded in getting the Commission of Inquiry into the Walwal incident really going, with the result that, as already stated, a finding was returned on 3 September, exonerating both parties. It further decided to meet again on 4 September to undertake the general examination of Italo-Ethiopian relations, and in the meantime delegated the negotiations on the major issue to a Three-Power Conference, consisting of Italy, France, and Great Britain. This Conference resulted in the submission of further proposals for a compromise to Signor Mussolini, which were summarily rejected by him on 18 August, and on the 21st Marshal de Bono received this laconic message: "Conferenza niente concluso; c'è Ginevra che concluderà lo stesso. Concludi."[1] When the Council met again on 4 September, the aggressive intentions of Italy were apparent to all. From this date until the outbreak of hostilities on 3 October, the proceedings at Geneva were practically continuous. On 11 September the British Foreign Secretary, Sir Samuel Hoare, made his memorable declaration of the intention of his country to fulfil its obligations under the Covenant. With the proviso that:

If risks for peace are to be run, they must be run by all. The security of the many cannot be assured by the efforts of a few, however powerful they may be,

he proceeded:

In conformity with its precise and explicit obligations the League stands, and my country stands with it, for the collective maintenance of the Covenant in its entirety, and particularly for steady and collective resistance to all acts of unprovoked aggression. The attitude of the British nation in the last few weeks has clearly demonstrated the fact that this is no variable and unreliable sentiment, but a principle of international conduct to which they and their Government hold with firm, enduring and universal persistence.

The demonstration of the attitude of the British people here referred to seems to be

[1] Conference settled nothing; Geneva will settle the same.

an allusion to an attempt to secure a pronouncement of public opinion on the question of the League and kindred matters, which had been organized, under the somewhat question-begging name of the "Peace Ballot," in the latter part of 1934. In this the public was asked to record its vote on the following questionnaire:

1. Should Great Britain remain a member of the League of Nations?
2. Are you in favour of an all-round reduction in armaments by international agreement?
3. Are you in favour of an all-round abolition of national military and naval aircraft by international agreement?
4. Should the manufacture and sale of armaments for private profit be prohibited by international agreement?
5. Do you consider that, if a nation insists on attacking another, the other nations should combine to compel it to stop by
   (a) Economic and non-military measures?
   (b) If necessary, military measures?

The implication in the title — that an affirmative vote was for peace, and presumably a negative one for war — is perhaps deserving of criticism, and all the questions except the first postulated the existence of a degree of international agreement and collaboration, the difficulty of ensuring which was in fact the crux of the whole problem. Granted "international agreement," and the combination of "the other nations" on which question 5 depended, British statesmen of all parties, whether in 1935 or later, could with a clear conscience have returned an affirmative answer to every question except the fourth, which was more controversial and open to objection, but does not concern us here. The fifth question may be further criticized on the ground that it assumes the possibility of applying economic sanctions without an ultimate willingness to back them with force.

On 27 June 1935, the results were announced. The total votes cast reached the impressive figure of 11,559,165. Over eleven million answered the first question affirmatively. Over ten million did the same for questions 2, 4, and 5a, while the affirmative vote on No. 3 was not much lower. There was, however, a highly significant drop in the answers to 5b, and those who approved military sanctions were only 6,784,368, though even this showed a striking majority over the negative vote of 2,351,981. Regarded, therefore, in the light of a mandate to the British Government, on a critical occasion, the voice of the plebiscite may fairly be said to have been: "Go as far as you can, in combination with other members, to secure and observe loyalty to the Covenant, and to resist aggression; but do all you can to keep out of war, even in company with other member-States; and we give no support at all to military measures which will fall exclusively or preponderantly on British shoulders." The policy subsequently followed by the British Government is exposed to criticism from a number of standpoints, especially from that of its intrinsic soundness as a way of dealing with the situation, but there is a good case for saying that it conformed closely to the above prescription. By treating the sanctions dealt with in question 5 as an open question independent of No. 1, the "Peace Ballot" clearly drew a distinction, whether rightly or wrongly, between remaining a member of the League of Nations and remaining bound by the obligations of the Covenant. Its promoters are therefore estopped from relying on a breach of Article 10 — an issue which they never laid before the public — or from insisting on the letter of the law as laid down in Article 16. The "Peace Ballot" is merely mentioned here as a fact in the history of the Abyssinian crisis, indicating the current trend of British opinion: it should not, in the writer's opinion, be regarded, as it has been, as something which the National Government, in the ensuing election in November, accepted and then betrayed.

On 3 October 1935, the expected act of Italian aggression took place, and on the 7th the Council of the League, its members voting individually by roll-call, unanimously except for the vote of the delinquent, adopted a report declaring that Italy had resorted to war in breach of the Covenant. In the ensuing meeting of the Assembly, on 11 October, fifty States members concurred in the view adopted by the Council, Switzerland made a reservation with regard to its participation in sanctions, while Austria, Hungary, and Albania, owing to their special relations with the transgressor, declared their dissent. The problem of recommending and co-ordinating the sanctions to be imposed was entrusted to a committee, and it was immediately decided to raise the arms embargo previously imposed by some nations upon Abyssinia and to impose a similar embargo against Italy (Proposal 1). A comprehensive financial sanction was also at once imposed (Proposal 2), and the acceptance of imports from Italy was immediately afterwards prohibited (Proposal 3). Finally, a very limited embargo on the export to Italy of certain important supplies came into force on 18 November. From this the most important omission was oil, which was excluded ostensibly on the ground that the list was confined to commodities controlled by League Powers.

Though some surprise was expressed at the fact that the rusty sanctions machinery of the League had at last been set in motion, the most that was done fell lamentably short of the complete and general boycott visualized by the founders of the League, or indeed of the minimum obligations under the letter of the Covenant. For by Article 16 all members of the League

undertake *immediately* to subject (the delinquent State) to the severance of all trade or financial relations, *the prohibition of all intercourse between their nationals and the nationals of the Covenant-breaking State*, and the *prevention of all financial, commercial or personal intercourse between the nationals of the Covenant-breaking State and the nationals of any other State, whether a Member of the League or not.*

Very little of this was done. It must be remembered, however, that the leading Powers concerned — England and France — were determined from the first to avoid putting such pressure upon Italy as might involve them in war. On the day preceding his historic speech at Geneva Sir Samuel Hoare had consulted with M. Laval, with a result which the latter professed to understand as follows:

We found ourselves instantaneously in agreement upon ruling out military sanctions, not adopting any measure of naval blockade, never contemplating the closure of the Suez Canal — in a word, ruling out everything that might lead to war.

Though this interpretation was incorrect, and Sir Samuel at no time pledged himself permanently to exclude military sanctions, the obvious unwillingness of France to co-operate to such an extent placed at once practically the whole burden of any such measures upon Great Britain, and threatened to convert collective into individual action. The situation with which both of these Powers was confronted was, in fact, a very difficult one. Italy had thrown down a challenge to the League, the non-acceptance of which might be fatal to its continued existence, and would in any case be a most serious blow to its prestige. To France the League had always been an instrument of *European* security and organization. To most English statesmen the League was an institution almost essential, under present-day conditions, for carrying on the traditional lines of British foreign policy in regard to Europe. The course marked out for Great Britain in Europe has almost always been a combination of the mediatory role for which her external position fits her, with the preservation of a multiple balance of power nearly incompatible with fixed alliances. Isolation, if ever practicable, is regarded in all responsible quarters as impossible today; with isolation and fixed alliances thus ruled out, England turned naturally to the support of an institution which, like herself, promoted a multiple balance and opposed the steps leading to the hegemony of a single Power, while at the same time it afforded unrivalled facilities for mediation. The view, generally entertained on the Continent, that in the Abyssinian crisis Great Britain was manipulating the League in her own special interests, was of course quite unfounded in the sense in which the imputation was made, but it is none the less true that, in wishing to preserve the League against the dangers now threatening it, England was not actuated by a vague and altruistic idealism, but by a most realistic desire to maintain an instrument vital to her own traditional policy.

But there were some considerations which militated against firm action in the situation which had now arisen. The first was the military and naval weakness of Great Britain, owing to the extent to which she had disarmed. A second was the necessity of correlating British policy with that of France. A third was the advisability of retaining as large a combination as possible to control the actions of Germany. And finally, there was the fact that the League was a means to an end, that end being above all things the prevention of a general war, such as is almost inevitable when war breaks out between the Great Powers of Europe. To use the means of the League, *á outrance,* for the defence of Abyssinian integrity, involved the only conceivable immediate risk of the precise catastrophe which the League was created to avert.

It was in this dilemma that the policy adopted in the Abyssinian crisis fell hopelessly between two stools and met with complete disaster. There was something to be said for a "European" attitude which refused to intervene at all, and frankly explained why. There was much to be said for a resolve to save Abyssinia — and the League — at all costs. There was little enough to be said for the imposition of innocuous sanctions, which the aggressor, though none the less irritated, could modify at his pleasure by the threat of war.

This might well have been evident but for an erroneous estimate of the Italian prospects. The preponderant expert opinion of soldiers and travellers was inclined to believe that the difficulties of climate and terrain would prove insuperable to the Italian forces, and that Italy was either faced with defeat or at any rate with a long war, in which even the mildest sanctions might have time to play a decisive part. Mr. Chamberlain, who at this time was among the members of the Cabinet most heartily in support of a vigorous policy, went even farther, and recorded in his private diary, on 8 December, the view that: "by putting his great army the other side the Suez Canal, Mussolini has tied a noose round his own neck, and left the end hanging out for anyone with a Navy to pull." This belief affected different categories of opinion in different ways. The British public rejoiced, and was not in the least inclined to do anything to extricate Signor Mussolini from what they took to be his awkward predicament. To the French, on the other hand, the defeat of the Italians meant simply ruining the prestige and permanently estranging the sympathies of a hardly won and valued ally. They could not in the least understand the apparently new-born enthusiasm of England for this particular experiment in collective security. For years they had implored Great Britain to play an effective part in the only security which mattered in their estimation, and to pledge herself unmistakably to maintain the integrity of their friends in eastern Europe. All in vain. But just when, at a most critical juncture, Italy had been won over into the camp of the faithful, England chose to direct against precisely that country a hitherto unsuspected zeal for the policy she had previously refused to promote. France could not appreciate the distinction, so important to the British mind, between a concrete case and an abstract principle. For herself, the present crisis left her torn between rival anxieties. None valued the security side of the Covenant — for use in Europe *bien entendu* — more

than she; it was all to the good that the determination of the League to resort to sanctions should be demonstrated, but, now that the demonstration had been made, she wanted to save the face and keep the favour of her new ally as well. Let there be a happy ending — a settlement by mutual consent. Let the husks of the sanctionist regime induce just sufficient hunger in the prodigal to tempt him home to a liberal provision of some one else's fatted calf. Thus a grateful and not altogether discredited Mussolini could restore his support to a League which would have established a useful precedent of at least partial victory to deter future and more dangerous aggressors.

As for Sir Samuel Hoare, he found himself in the position of the leader of a charge exposed in no-man's land with his troop refusing to follow. If Italy were faced with defeat, she would rather go down fighting the champions of the League than face the ignominy of a second Adowa, brought about by a shortage of supplies. And, when she turned to look for the League's forces in the field, she would find only those of Great Britain.

We alone have taken these military precautions. There is the British fleet in the Mediterranean, there are the British reinforcements in Egypt, in Malta and Aden. Not a ship, not a machine, not a man has been moved by any other member State.

The hollow pretence, as Sir Samuel viewed it, of collective resistance would be exposed when the struggle turned into a duel between just two nations. In these circumstances, after the apparent failure of his original trumpet call, he was induced, in common with the League as a whole, to adopt M. Laval's specious argument that it was the duty of that institution, after as well as before the act of Italian aggression, to pursue the policies of coercion and mediation simultaneously. The argument was indeed more characteristic of British than it was of French thought, since it was as a forum of international negotiation rather than a potential alliance marshalled against aggressors that the League had from the first been valued by British politicians, and it was probably accepted with more sincerity by Sir Samuel than by M. Laval. In view of current misconceptions of British Government policy, it should be emphasized that there is no reason to doubt the sincerity of Sir Samuel's conviction that the step which he was about to take was that best calculated to preserve the influence and prestige of the League itself, and that this was his main objective. In his own words:

We had no fear as a nation of any Italian threats. . . . What was in our mind was something very different, that an isolated attack of this kind launched upon one Power without . . . the full support of the other Powers would, it seemed to me, almost inevitably lead to the dissolution of the League.

In the light of what actually occurred, we have all grown so used to attributing the death of the League to a flagrant sacrifice of principle in its endeavour to achieve a settlement that we are apt to forget that it was equally possible, as Sir Samuel contended, for its authority to be finally destroyed by a situation which revealed unmistakably the pasteboard composition of the Don Quixote's helmet of military sanctions. There was also, no doubt, a secondary consideration. We could defeat Italy, but what if another enemy seized the opportunity of exploiting the reduced and battered condition of our navy?

The reader may observe, as a further possible point in extenuation of British Government policy, the strength of the bargaining position occupied by M. Laval. In complaining of the isolated situation of Great Britain, Sir Samuel obviously implied, in particular, the defection or hesitation of France, on whom, as the only other Great Power capable of affording effective naval assistance in the Mediterranean, Great Britain primarily relied in

the event of a trial of force. With French co-operation, his argument clearly lost its validity. The weakness of our situation really lay in the necessity for keeping step with France, a circumstance which gave M. Laval an invaluable lever in his task of exacting British acquiescence in his schemes.

Such was the background of the notorious Laval-Hoare "peace proposal" of December 1935. The urgent necessity, in the opinion of the authors, for such a plan was due to the imminence of a proposal for the imposition of an "oil-sanction." It was the view of Sir Samuel Hoare that if

the non-member states took an effective part in it, the oil embargo might have such an effect upon the hostilities as to force their termination.

The co-operation of the United States at least seemed at this time a possibility, and, in spite of the blocking and procrastinating tactics of M. Laval, the project was shortly due to come up for final consideration, and the orator of 11 September

did not feel . . . justified in proposing any postponement of the embargo, unless it could be shown to the League that negotiations had actually started.

He was on the point of seeking a much-needed holiday in Switzerland when M. Laval on 7 December, secured his approval of a plan which, stripped of its euphemistic clothing as an "Exchange of Territories" and a "Zone of Economic Expansion and Settlement," meant the buying off of Signor Mussolini by conceding to him territory and virtual control of far wider extent than he had so far won by the sword. As an attempt to rescue Abyssinia from complete annihilation, it might perhaps have been justified, but in fact it was put forward at a time when no such debacle was anticipated. Sir Samuel himself predicted a long and indecisive struggle, followed by a compromised settlement. The proposal was obviously put forward in the interests of policy the British Government met with no perceptible opposition from the public opinion of the country. On 6 July the Co-ordinating Committee of the League recommended that sanctions should be dropped as from 15 July. The experiment in practical collective security had finally broken down.

Some days earlier, the seven States of the so-called Oslo group — Sweden, Norway, Denmark, Finland, Holland, Belgium, and Luxembourg — had drawn from the situation the conclusion, which they embodied in a joint communiqué, that, so long as conditions remained as at present, they would not consider themselves bound by the provisions of Article 16 of the Covenant, and from this point the Scandinavians at any rate swung back to their traditional policy of neutrality.

The Abyssinian crisis may perhaps be thought to have been given an amount of space disproportionate to a work of this description. The justification lies in the fact that it marks a crucial turning-point in post-war history. The triumph of Italian aggression, naked and unashamed, affected the whole world with fundamental consequences. To England, it meant the virtual destruction of the institution which successive Governments, of different parties, had proclaimed to be the keystone of their foreign policy. To France, as will appear in the next chapter, it meant that the enemy of whom she stood most in terror was encouraged to fresh audacity and rescued from his previous isolation. And finally, to the Italian transgressor, by an act of poetic justice, it was destined to mean the extinction of his influence on the Danube, and the arrival of German forces on the Brenner.

Powers pledged to the maintenance of Ethiopian integrity, rather than in those of Abyssinia. It was in fact a "peace plan" on the lines of that for which the Great Powers had been satirized by an Oxford poet towards the end of the nineteenth century:

Be it yours to assuage for inadequate wage our
  unseemly contentions and quarrels;
Be it yours to maintain your respectable reign
  in the sphere of Political Morals;
And, relying no more on the shedding of gore
  or the rule of torpedoes and sabres,
Make beneficent plots for dividing in lots the
  domains of your paralyzed neighbours!

Having thus provisionally agreed to what he regarded as a proposal ripe for further consideration by the British Cabinet and the League, Sir Samuel dispatched the results of his conference to London and proceeded on his holiday to Switzerland. The understanding was that the plan should remain a profound secret until such further consideration had taken place, but in fact it was immediately disclosed to the French press through what we may now confidently attribute to a deliberate breach of faith on the part of M. Laval. He felt, no doubt, that such premature disclosure would force the hand of the British Cabinet by bringing into play their loyalty to an absent colleague, and this calculation proved correct. Though admittedly unhappy and dissatisfied about the terms, the Cabinet gave the project a reluctant assent, and on 10 December a telegram was sent to Addis Ababa, urging the Emperor "to give careful and favourable consideration to these proposals and on no account to lightly reject them." That the terms were not regarded as final is indicated by the fact that the message further spoke of "the opportunity of negotiation which they afford."

But M. Laval had not reckoned with the forces of British public opinion. The plan, thus disclosed, and illustrated in the press by a map showing that apparently two-thirds of Ethiopia were to be awarded

to the aggressor, was immediately met a storm of indignant protest from the ish public and the newly elected rank file of Government supporters. In the cent electoral campaign the latter had stantly and sincerely repudiated the f cast of Government intentions expressed a work hastily brought out for the occas by a band of opposition students of int national affairs:

They reckon on the General Election de nitely giving them the upper hand in th Conservative Party, with a blank cheque t arm to the teeth as well as freeing them fron the fear of public opinion. *Then they will d a deal with their friend Mussolini,* and after that launch out on the "new foreign policy" about which the Government Press have been hinting for some time. That policy in their view is either to say that the League has failed altogether or that it needs drastic reform by dropping Articles 10 and 16 from the Covenant, and in either case to plunge with a vengeance into the game of alliances and power politics.

In the light of what had now transpired, they felt, with shame, that they had won the election under false pretences. The Government bent to the storm, and Sir Samuel Hoare was replaced at the Foreign Office by Mr. Eden. The plan was dead, but its ghost continued to haunt the nations who had hitherto reposed confidence in the protection of the League. The harm was irrevocably done.

In any case, the pessimistic view of the Italian prospects proved to be mistaken. Unable to secure adequate supplies of arms, subjected from the air to a rain of mustard gas against which they were altogether unprotected, and defective in their strategy and tactics, the Abyssinian forces met with much earlier and more decisive defeat than anyone had anticipated. On 2 May 1936, the Emperor left the country, and three days later the Italian forces were in occupation of his capital. In the following month there was a very general movement for the abandonment of sanctions, in which

A TALE OF SIN AND NEMESIS

ARNOLD J. TOYNBEE

The famed philosopher-historian has been professor of international history at the University of London since 1925. Toynbee is the leading exponent in the English language of the cyclical theory of history, of the rise and fall of civilizations, a view which is propounded at length in his eleven-volume *A Study of History* (London, 1935–59). From 1920 to 1938 he annually reviewed the events of the year in *A Survey of International Affairs* published under the auspices of the Royal Institute of International Affairs. The following is the introduction to the survey of the Ethiopian Crisis in 1935.

THE tragic episode of international history which is recorded in this volume is a tale of sin and nemesis. Even at the moment of writing, on the very morrow of the events, the historian could offer this bald interpretation of the plot with some confidence that his reading of its outlines would not be disputed either by contemporary participants and observers or by a yet unborn Posterity. There was, however, perhaps room for some difference of opinion in the identification of the actors who were impersonating—beneath the conventional tragic mask—the stock characters of hero and villain and victim.

Was the play that was being performed in the arena of the oecumenical amphitheatre in A.D. 1935–6 a tragedy in the Ancient Greek style, with a single soul—raised by Fate to a pinnacle of power—seen succumbing to the sin of *hybris* and being overtaken by the nemesis of *atê*? If this was the play, then the protagonist could only be Benito Mussolini. Or was it rather a tragedy in the vein of a modern Western Society which was relapsing into the collectivism of the ant-heap and the beehive? If that was the deeper meaning of this awful spectacle, then the little men — Mussolinis and Lavals and Hoares and Baldwins — who were wearing the masks and buskins, executing the gestures and speaking the lines on the stage, were mere mannikin-puppets, like the Bagrations and Napoleons of Tolstoy's *War and Peace* or Hardy's *The Dynasts*. The true protagonist, on this view, would be, not the soul of Benito Mussolini, but the Society of Western Christendom, and the sin which was evoking nemesis would be, not the personal *hybris* of an individual, but the social *karma* of the Old Adam — a heritage of Original Sin which had been accumulating through many generations.

Was it, then, the Romagnol dictator or the Great Society of a Westernized World that was the true protagonist in this performance of a traditional plot? If the historian were the Duce's confessor, it would evidently be his duty to regard the whole vast transaction as the personal action of Signor Mussolini; and from this angle of vision the Duce's decision (whenever it was taken) to launch Italy upon a war of aggression against Abyssinia was doubtless a mortal sin which the sinner would have

From Arnold J. Toynbee, *Survey of International Affairs 1935*, Vol. II (London, 1936), pp. 1–8. Published on behalf of the Royal Institute of International Affairs. Reprinted by permission of Oxford University Press.

to expiate either in this world or in another. If, however, the historian happened to be a student of public affairs who was an Englishman and a British subject, it would ill become him to cajole his own conscience by making a Mussolini his scapegoat; for from an English standpoint — if the English observer viewed the spectacle with open eyes and honest mind — it was impossible to see the tragedy solely in terms of the *hybris* of Mussolini or, for that matter, of a totalitarian Fascist Italy. From an English standpoint the Mussolinian sin of commission — the positive, strong-willed, aggressive egotism which had tempted the Italian war-lord into committing a crime of violence in breach of all his covenants — was inextricably interwoven with a complementary sin of omission: a negative, weak-willed, cowardly egotism which had tempted the reigning politicians in Great Britain and France — in deference to what they believed to be the will of their constituents — to stop short of an effective fulfilment of their own covenants because they flinched from the risks and sacrifices to which their countries stood pledged to expose themselves in the cause of international justice and law and order. While Signor Mussolini had not the patience and imagination to abide by his promises to promote Italy's legitimate national interests by none other than peaceful means, his French and British fellow actors had not the virtues requisite for whole-heartedly putting into practice the nobler and wiser policy to which they were paying, all the time, a perfunctory lip service. Their professed intention — if their adherence to the Covenant of the League of Nations and to the Kellogg-Briand Pact was to be taken seriously — was to establish a reign of law and order in the international arena by making a reality of both the twin pillars of Justice: Collective Security and Peaceful Change. Yet, when their sincerity was put to a supreme test through an Italian challenge (at first plaintive and finally truculent) in the seventeen post-war years that ended in 1935, the French and English did

not muster up either the generosity and imagination to make a success of Peaceful Change or the courage and imagination to make a success of Collective Security. They neither responded in 1920 to Signor Tittoni's plea for an equitable distribution of raw materials nor restrained Signor Mussolini in 1935 from launching an aggressive war against Abyssinia.

In this light it is apparent that the sin which was committed in 1935 was not merely Mussolini's or Fascismo's or Italy's. This guilt was shared by Britain and France, and in some measure by the whole living generation of the Western Society — for example, by the contemporary Canadians whose gentle spokesman had inflicted at Geneva, in 1920, a diplomatic defeat upon the Italians' timid spokesman, Signor Tittoni. Nor was it only the living generation of the Western Society that was implicated, for Signor Mussolini came nearest to justifying his own crime and to putting the sanction-taking Powers out of countenance when he proclaimed that, in seeking to acquire an overseas empire by force of arms, the Italians were simply doing in the twentieth century what the British and French had done in the nineteenth and eighteenth centuries, the Dutch and Swedes in the seventeenth century, and the Spaniards and Portuguese in the sixteenth.

On this wider, and perhaps also deeper, view, Signor Mussolini's deliberate personal sin might be almost eclipsed by his involuntary historical rôle of exposing the moral perversity of the once Christian society which had confessed its apostasy in the act of raising him to power. The perversity of the modern Western ideal of Nationalism was shown up by an Italian Imperialism which was the aftermath of an Italian *Risorgimento*. The perversity of the modern Western intellectual feat of Physical Science was shown up by the application of chemistry and aeronautics to the devilish device of spraying poison gas from the air. The perversity of the modern Western commercial spirit — a worship of Mammon from which the nineteenth-century philosophers had naïvely expected a redemption of the World — was shown up by the greed with which (after, as well as before, the application of economic sanctions against Italy) the businessmen of even the best behaved and most brightly enlightened countries of the Western World rushed in to make their profit by catering for the aggressor's military requirements.

If we try to marshal the several participants in the tragedy in their order of merit, we shall find that the poorest figure was cut by those with the most specious claim to represent the fine flower of Western culture.

The *beau rôle* was played by the Emperor Haile Selassie, the heir of a non-Western Christian tradition, who combined an antique virtue with an enlightened modernism without either relapsing into the truculent barbarism of his own predecessor Theodore or sliding into the unprincipled rascality of a twentieth-century Chinese war-lord. The second prize might be awarded to the Emperor's Amhara warriors — who knew how to die like Spartans, though they might not know how to fight like Pathans — and these military honours might be divided between the Lion of Judah's whelps and their African antagonists — Eritrean and Libyan Askaris — who fought with an equal bravery in a fratricidal war into which they had been hounded by the avarice and ambition of Italian empire-builders who were only taking a leaf out of a French and English book when they trained their non-European subjects to fight their battles for them.

Of all the Europeans who were concerned in the African war of 1935–6 the most respectable were the Italian workmen, who performed prodigies of labour in building motor-roads at an extraordinary pace over an intractable terrain. Even the Italian soldiers, who submitted to being mobilized and sent to march and climb over trackless Ethiopian mountains under a tropical sun, deserve their meed of praise; and so do the majority of their countrymen who stayed at home; for these, too, followed their leader in a war (which, as they saw it, was defensive as well as bloodless) against a barrage of sanctions (a new-fangled weapon which was nerve-racking just because it was intangible). As for Signor Mussolini, he never responded to the Emperor's challenge to meet him in the field; yet he showed a moral courage (for the like of which many English people were looking in vain to their constitutionally appointed Government) in sending half a million Italians to conduct a difficult military campaign on the farther side of the Suez Canal when the British Fleet was concentrated in the Levant, while fifty-two states had agreed to cooperate in frustrating Mussolini's military aims by imposing on Italy at any rate a partial economic boycott. In virtue of this courage, for what it was worth, the Italian dictator cut at least a more heroic figure than the politicians and the electorates of Great Britain and France, upon whom History would perhaps pass the laconic verdict that they failed to do their duty — though they had no title to claim invincible ignorance of what this duty was, and would also find it difficult to prove that here duty was in conflict with self-interest (unless self-interest were to be interpreted as a sheer licence to sacrifice the welfare of to-morrow to the ease of to-day).

In this common feebleness the French showed a greater frankness, though not any greater nobility or sharper vision, than their English neighbours. The French made no concealment of their naïvely unprincipled hope that they might be able to sabotage the application of the Covenant against Italy in order to preserve this self-same Covenant intact for future use against Germany — with a triumphant Italian Covenant-breaker helping France, in the name of the Covenant, to hold Germany in check! The English, for their part, desired to do what they had pledged themselves to do for the vindication of international law and order, and they also believed that honesty was actually the best policy for the British Empire in this case; but at the same time they made a stipulation with themselves that neither Justice nor Expediency were to be ensued to a point at which they might entail any serious risk or sacrifice in which the whole, or even the major part, of the burden would fall upon the United Kingdom.

The electorate of the United Kingdom was less clear-sighted and self-conscious in this matter than the politicians who were soliciting their votes; but, by the same token, the electorate might also be judged to be more sincere. A vein of insincerity appeared to reveal itself in the behaviour of prominent members of "the National Government" in at least three test cases which arose in the course of the calendar year 1935. The first case was the abrupt change of tone towards "the Peace Ballot" as soon as it became apparent that it was proving a success; the second case was the contrast between the compact which Sir Samuel Hoare made in private with Monsieur Laval at Geneva on the 10th September and the speech which he delivered in public in the Assembly of the League of Nations on the following day; the third case was the apparent inconsistency between the platform on which the "National" coalition won a general election on the 14th November and the terms of "the Laval-Hoare Peace Plan" in which Mr. Baldwin and his colleagues acquiesced within fourteen days of meeting the newly elected parliament with a majority that ensured an extension of their tenure of office. The leaders and partisans of "the National Government" also struck a note which, besides sounding hollow, might perhaps be criticized as impolitic when they persistently commended themselves to the electorate for their determination to keep the country out of war while they were in the act of rearming.

Since Great Britain and France, between them, were still, at this time, the hub of the Western universe, these symptoms of political feebleness in these two countries were serious portents for the general destiny of the Western Society. At a time when the parochialism of the latest age was rapidly being turned into an anachronism by the forced march of technical progress, it might confidently be assumed that the destiny of this society was some form of social and political unification by some means or other. At the same time there were two alternative routes to that single and therefore inevitable goal; and it looked as though this choice of means for arriving at an inexorable end might make the whole difference between social catastrophe and social welfare.

One way towards the unification of the World would be for the British Commonwealth of Nations, in collaboration with France and with a number of other liberal-minded communities, to build itself into a League of Nations constituted on the democratic pattern and informed with the democratic spirit, and to lay stone on stone — never ceasing from mental strife nor letting the sword sleep in the hand — until this voluntary association should have become substantially secure and approximately world-wide. This was, indeed, the enterprise to which the United Kingdom and France, on emerging from the ordeal of 1914–18, had officially dedicated themselves in company with all their fellow states members of the then inaugurated League; and when once their intuition had thus prompted them to take the tide of Destiny at the flood, they had started on their voyage with the fairest prospect of its leading on to Fortune. Yet at the time of writing in 1936, which was the eighteenth year of this post-war international voyage of political exploration, the prospect was dismally blighted and the heavens were gloomily overcast. At this moment it looked as though the strain of "making the World safe for Democracy" by force of arms had broken the nerve of the official victors in the last General War, and broken it so seriously that they were now finding themselves morally incapable of making the lesser efforts and taking the slighter risks that must still be faced if the true harvest of the victory of 1918 was to be triumphantly gathered in.[1] This apparent failure of nerve was the more extraordinary in view of the penalty which it threatened to entail — a penalty which was so appalling and so imminent that it could hardly be overlooked or ignored. In effect, the French and English in 1935–6 were confronted with a choice between making the post-war system of law and order genuinely work or else seeing the frail structure relapse into the chaotic anarchy which had begotten not only the war of 1914–18 but one war behind another before that. If, with this choice before them, the two leading democratic nations of Western Europe did irrevocably fail to rise to the occasion, then History would assuredly pronounce upon their fatal default the verdict that

No man having put his hand to the plough and looking back is fit for the Kingdom of God.

If the oecumenical society of this generation was not destined to achieve its inevitable political unification along the path of voluntary co-operation in the shape of the League of Nations, what was the alternative route by which it was condemning itself to travel? That route was clearly indicated when a young English airwoman succeeded in flying from Croydon to Capetown in 78½ hours a few days after a number of young Italian airmen — only a few hours' flying distance away from the Central African section of her course — had been engaged in spraying poison gas from their planes in order to break the *morale* of a warlike nation which had hitherto managed to maintain its independence against all comers over a period of at least two thousand years. In the synchronism between these two feats of aircraft, the destiny of Society was written on the skies for all to read there. If the World was not to

be unified politically by a voluntary agreement, it was manifestly destined to have its inevitable unity imposed upon it by a violence armed with the full powers of the latest Western technique. And it was idle to scout this prospect on the ground that human beings would shrink from turning these terrible powers to account for the perpetration of murder on so vast a scale, or again on the ground that the enterprise of unifying the World by force would prove to be beyond the strength of even the most potent and ruthless and unscrupulous war-lord. Such *a priori* arguments were refuted in advance by the testimony of History; for History bore witness that, whenever men found themselves at war, they invariably made weapons out of every instrument at their command, and she also preserved the record of at least a dozen instances in which a society that was ripe for political unification had been unified by military force, even when the empire-building militarists had disposed of only a modest fund of technique. The classic example of such unification through military conquest was called to mind by Signor Mussolini's conceit of reviving the Roman Empire; and while it was improbable that the oecumenical empire in which the Roman Empire would find its counterpart in the modern World would be established by Fascist Italy, it was not impossible that, in striking down the League of Nations, the head of the Italian state was opening the door to world-power (a veritable *ianua leti*) for some mightier competitor in the shape of a National-Socialist Germany or a Communist Russia.

This was the vista which was opened up in A.D. 1936 by the French and British peoples' apparent failure of nerve and hankering for release from responsibility even at the price of abdication; and in this light it was they, rather than Signor Mussolini, who were to be regarded as the central figures in the current act of the international drama. For that reason the writer of this Survey has addressed himself . . . to his own countrymen and not to the Italian dictator.

---

[1] This had been the fate of Holland in the eighteenth century, after her victory in her heroic struggle against Louis XIV from A.D. 1672 to A.D. 1713. In A.D. 1936 it looked as though both the United Kingdom and France might now, in their turn, be on the point of retiring from the international arena, as Holland and Sweden and Spain and Portugal had all retired in their turn.

THE GATHERING STORM—SANCTIONS AGAINST ITALY

WINSTON CHURCHILL

Winston Churchill was at the time of the Italian-Ethiopian Crisis a spirited critic of governmental policy, although his own Conservative Party was then in office under Stanley Baldwin. His role as a Cassandra is nowhere more brilliantly recorded than in his own account in the first volume of his general history of the Second World War, which he wrote after the Labour victory at the polls in 1945. Churchill's eyes were pinned upon the rise of Nazi Germany. It is important, however, to follow closely his realistic position in regard to Italy.

Ever since the Stresa Conference, Mussolini's preparations for the conquest of Abyssinia had been apparent. It was evident that British opinion would be hostile to such an act of Italian aggression. Those of us who saw in Hitler's Germany a danger, not only to peace but to survival, dreaded this movement of a first-class Power, as Italy was then rated, from our side to the other. I remember a dinner at which Sir Robert Vansittart and Mr. Duff Cooper, then only an under-secretary, were present, at which this adverse change in the balance of Europe was clearly foreseen. The project was mooted of some of us going out to see Mussolini in order to explain to him the inevitable effects which would be produced in Great Britain. Nothing came of this; nor would it have been of any good. Mussolini, like Hitler, regarded Britannia as a frightened, flabby old woman, who at the worst would only bluster and was, anyhow, incapable of making war. Lord Lloyd, who was on friendly terms with him, noted how he had been struck by the Joad Resolution of the Oxford undergraduates in 1933 refusing "to fight for king and country."

*   *   *

In Parliament I expressed my misgivings on July 11:

We seemed to have allowed the impression to be created that we were ourselves coming forward as a sort of bell-wether or fugleman to lead opinion in Europe against Italy's Abyssinian designs. It was even suggested that we would act individually and independently. I am glad to hear from the Foreign Secretary that there is no foundation for that. We must do our duty, but we must do it with other nations only in accordance with the obligations which others recognize as well. We are not strong enough to be the lawgiver and the spokesman of the world. We will do our part, but we cannot be asked to do more than our part in these matters. . . .

As we stand today there is no doubt that a cloud has come over the old friendship between Great Britain and Italy, a cloud which, it seems to me, may very easily not pass away, although undoubtedly it is everyone's desire that it should. It is an old friendship, and we must not forget, what is a little-known fact,

From Winston Churchill, *Second World War, The Gathering Storm*, pp. 167–170, 172–187. By permission of and arrangement with Houghton Mifflin Company, Boston, and Cassell & Company, London. Copyright, 1948.

In spite of my anxieties about Germany, and little as I liked the way our affairs were handled, I remember being stirred by this speech when I read it in Riviera sunshine. It aroused everyone, and reverberated throughout the United States. It united all those forces in Britain which stood for a fearless combination of righteousness and strength. Here at least was a policy. If only the orator had realized what tremendous powers he held unleashed in his hand at that moment, he might indeed for a while have led the world.

These declarations gathered their validity from the fact that they had behind them, like many causes which in the past have proved vital to human progress and freedom, the British Navy. For the first and the last time the League of Nations seemed to have at its disposal a secular arm. Here was the international police force, upon the ultimate authority of which all kinds of diplomatic and economic pressures and persuasion could be employed. When on September 12, the very next day, the battle cruisers *Hood* and *Renown*, accompanied by the Second Cruiser Squadron and a destroyer flotilla, arrived at Gibraltar, it was assumed on all sides that Britain would back her words with deeds. Policy and action alike gained immediate and overwhelming support at home. It was taken for granted, not unnaturally, that neither the declaration nor the movement of warships would have been made without careful expert calculation by the Admiralty of the fleet or fleets required in the Mediterranean to make our undertakings good.

At the end of September, I had to make a speech at the City Carlton Club, an orthodox body of some influence. I tried to convey a warning to Mussolini which I believe he read. . . . Sir Austen Chamberlain wrote to me agreeing with this speech, and I replied:

October 1, 1935.

I am glad you approve the line I took about Abyssinia; but I am very unhappy. It would be a terrible deed to smash up Italy,

and it will cost us dear. How strange it is that after all these years of begging France to make it up with Italy, we are now forcing her to choose between Italy and ourselves! I do not think we ought to have taken the lead in such a vehement way. If we had felt so strongly on the subject we should have warned Mussolini two months before. The sensible course would have been gradually to strengthen the Fleet in the Mediterranean during the early summer, and so let him see how grave the matter was. Now what can he do? I expect a very serious rise of temperature when the fighting [in Abyssinia] begins.

* * *

In October, Mussolini, undeterred by belated British naval movements, launched the Italian armies upon the invasion of Abyssinia. On the tenth, by the votes of fifty sovereign states to one, the Assembly of the League resolved to take collective measures against Italy, and a committee of eighteen was appointed to make further efforts for a peaceful solution. Mussolini, thus confronted, made a clear-cut statement, marked by deep shrewdness. Instead of saying, "Italy will meet sanctions with war," he said: "Italy will meet them with discipline, with frugality, and with sacrifice." At the same time, however, he intimated that *he would not tolerate the imposition of any sanctions which hampered his invasion of Abyssinia.* If that enterprise were endangered, he would go to war with whoever stood in his path. "Fifty nations!" he said. "Fifty nations, led by one!" Such was the position in the weeks which preceded the dissolution of Parliament in Britain and the general election, which was not constitutionally due.

* * *

Bloodshed in Abyssinia, hatred of Fascism, the invocation of sanctions by the League, produced a convulsion within the British Labour Party. Trade-unionists, among whom Mr. Ernest Bevin was outstanding, were by no means pacifist by temperament. A very strong desire to fight the Italian Dictator, to enforce sanctions of that at the time Italy entered into the Triple Alliance in the last century she stipulated particularly that in no circumstances would her obligations under the alliance bring her into armed conflict with Great Britain.

* * *

In August, the Foreign Secretary invited me and also the Opposition Party leaders to visit him separately at the Foreign Office, and the fact of these consultations was made public by the Government. Sir Samuel Hoare told me of this growing anxiety about Italian aggression against Abyssinia and asked me how far I should be prepared to go against it. Wishing to know more about the internal and personal situation at the Foreign Office under dyarchy before replying, I asked about Eden's view. "I will get him to come," said Hoare, and in a few minutes Anthony arrived smiling and in the best of tempers. We had an easy talk. I said I thought the Foreign Secretary was *justified in going as far with the League of Nations against Italy as he could carry France;* but I added that he ought not to put any pressure upon France because of her military convention with Italy and her German preoccupations; and that in the circumstances I did not expect France would go very far. I then spoke of the Italian divisions on the Brenner Pass, of the unguarded southern front of France and other military aspects.

Generally I strongly advised the Ministers not to try to take a leading part or to put themselves forward too prominently. In this I was, of course, oppressed by my German fears and the condition to which our defences had been reduced. . . .

* * *

As the summer drew on, the movement of Italian troopships through the Suez Canal was continuous, and considerable forces and supplies were assembled along the eastern Abyssinian frontier. Suddenly an extraordinary, and to me, after my talks at the Foreign Office, a quite unexpected, event occurred. On August 24, the Cabinet

resolved and declared that Britain w uphold its obligation under its treaties under the Covenant of the League. produced an immediate crisis in the M terranean, and I thought it right, sinc had been so recently consulted, to ask t Foreign Secretary to reassure me about t naval situation. . . .

* * *

Mr. Eden, Minister for League of Nations Affairs and almost co-equal of the Foreign Secretary, had already been for some weeks at Geneva, where he had rallied the Assembly to a policy of "sanctions" against Italy if she invaded Abyssinia. The peculiar office to which he had been appointed made him by its very nature concentrate upon the Abyssinian question with an emphasis which outweighed other aspects. "Sanctions" meant the cutting-off from Italy of all financial aid and of economic supplies, and the giving of all such assistance to Abyssinia. To a country like Italy, dependent for so many commodities needed in war upon unhampered imports from over-seas, this was indeed a formidable deterrent. Eden's zeal and address and the principles which he proclaimed dominated the Assembly. On September 11, the Foreign Secretary, Sir Samuel Hoare, having arrived at Geneva, himself addressed them:

I will begin by reaffirming the support of the League by the Government I represent and the interest of the British people in collective security. . . . The ideas enshrined in the Covenant and in particular the aspiration to establish the rule of law in international affairs have become a part of our national conscience. It is to the principles of the League and not to any particular manifestation that the British nation has demonstrated its adherence. Any other view is at once an underestimation of our good faith and an imputation upon our sincerity. In conformity with its precise and explicit obligations the League stands, and my country stands with it, for the collective maintenance of the Covenant in its entirety, and particularly for steady and collective resistance to all acts of unprovoked aggression.

a decisive character, and to use the British Fleet, if need be, surged through the sturdy wage-earners. Rough and harsh words were spoken at excited meetings. On one occasion Mr. Bevin complained that "he was tired of having George Lansbury's conscience carted about from conference to conference." Many members of the Parliamentary Labour Party shared the trade-union mood. In a far wider sphere, all the leaders of the League of Nations Union felt themselves bound to the cause of the League. Clause 5 of their "Peace Ballot" was plainly involved. Here were principles in obedience to which lifelong humanitarians were ready to die, and if to die, also to kill. On October 8, Mr. Lansbury resigned his leadership of the Parliamentary Labour Party, and Major Attlee, who had a fine war record, reigned in his stead.

*　*　*

But this national awakening was not in accord with Mr. Baldwin's outlook or intentions. It was not till several months after the election that I began to understand the principles upon which "sanctions" were founded. The Prime Minister had declared that sanctions meant war; secondly, he was resolved there must be no war; and thirdly, he decided upon sanctions. It was evidently impossible to reconcile these three conditions. Under the guidance of Britain and the pressures of Laval, the League of Nations Committee, charged with devising sanctions, kept clear of any that would provoke war. A large number of commodities, some of which were war materials, were prohibited from entering Italy, and an imposing schedule was drawn up. But oil, without which the campaign in Abyssinia could not have been maintained, continued to enter freely, because it was understood that to stop it meant war. Here the attitude of the United States, not a member of the League of Nations and the world's main oil supplier, though benevolent, was uncertain. Moreover, to stop it to Italy involved also stop-

ping it to Germany. The export of aluminum into Italy was strictly forbidden; but aluminum was almost the only metal that Italy produced in quantities beyond her own needs. The importation of scrap iron and iron ore into Italy was sternly vetoed in the name of public justice. But as the Italian metallurgical industry made but little use of them, and as steel billets and pig iron were not interfered with, Italy suffered no hindrance. Thus, the measures pressed with so great a parade were not real sanctions to paralyse the aggressor, but merely such half-hearted sanctions as the aggressor would tolerate, because in fact, though onerous, they stimulated Italian war spirit. The League of Nations, therefore, proceeded to the rescue of Abyssinia on the basis that nothing must be done to hamper the invading Italian armies. These facts were not known to the British public at the time of the election. They earnestly supported the policy of the sanctions, and believed that this was a sure way of bringing the Italian assault upon Abyssinia to an end.

Still less did His Majesty's Government contemplate the use of the Fleet. All kinds of tales were told of Italian suicide squadrons of dive-bombers which would hurl themselves upon the decks of our ships and blow them to pieces. The British Fleet which was lying at Alexandria had now been reinforced. It could by a gesture have turned back Italian transports from the Suez Canal, and would as a consequence have had to offer battle to the Italian Navy. We were told that it was not capable of meeting such an antagonist. I had raised the question at the outset, but had been reassured. Our battleships, of course, were old, and it now appeared that we had no aircraft cover and very little anti-aircraft ammunition. It transpired, however, that the Admiral commanding resented the suggestion attributed to him that he was not strong enough to fight a fleet action. It would seem that before taking their first decision to oppose the Italian aggression, His Majesty's Government should carefully have examined ways and means and also made up their minds.

There is no doubt on our present knowledge that a bold decision would have cut the Italian communications with Ethiopia, and that we should have been successful in any naval battle which might have followed. I was never in favour of isolated action by Great Britain, but having gone so far it was a grievous deed to recoil. Moreover, Mussolini would never have dared to come to grips with a resolute British Government. Nearly the whole of the world was against him, and he would have had to risk his régime upon a single-handed war with Britain, in which a fleet action in the Mediterranean would be the early and decisive test. How could Italy have fought this war? Apart from a limited advantage in modern light cruisers, her navy was but a fourth the size of the British. Her numerous conscript army, which was vaunted in millions, could not come into action. Her air power was in quantity and quality far below even our modest establishments. She would instantly have been blockaded. The Italian armies in Abyssinia would have famished for supplies and ammunition. Germany could as yet give no effective help. If ever there was an opportunity of striking a decisive blow in a generous cause with the minimum of risk, it was here and now. The fact that the nerve of the British Government was not equal to the occasion can be excused only by their sincere love of peace. Actually it played a part in leading to an infinitely more terrible war. Mussolini's bluff succeeded, and an important spectator drew farreaching conclusions from the fact. Hitler had long resolved on war for German aggrandisement. He now formed a view of Great Britain's degeneracy which was only to be changed too late for peace and too late for him. In Japan, also, there were pensive spectators.

* * *

The two opposite processes of gathering national unity on the burning issue of the hour and the clash of party interests inseparable from a general election moved forward together. This was greatly to the advantage of Mr. Baldwin and his supporters. "The League of Nations would remain as heretofore the keystone of British foreign policy," so ran the Government's election manifesto. "The prevention of war and the establishment of peace in the world must always be the most vital interest of the British people, and the League is the instrument which has been framed and to which we look for the attainment of these objects. We shall therefore continue to do all in our power to uphold the Covenant and to maintain and increase the efficiency of the League. In the present unhappy dispute between Italy and Abyssinia *there will be no wavering in the policy we have hitherto pursued.*"

The Labour Party, on the other hand, was much divided. The majority was pacifist, but Mr. Bevin's active campaign commanded many supporters among the masses. The official leaders, therefore, tried to give general satisfaction by pointing opposite ways at once. On the one hand they clamoured for decisive action against the Italian Dictator; on the other they denounced the policy of rearmament. Thus Mr. Attlee in the House of Commons on October 22: "We want effective sanctions, effectively applied. We support economic sanctions. We support the League system." But then, later in the same speech: "We are not persuaded that the way to safety is by piling up armaments. We do not believe that in this [time] there is such a thing as national defence. We think that you have to go forward to disarmament and not to the piling-up of armaments." Neither side usually has much to be proud of at election times. The Prime Minister himself was no doubt conscious of the growing strength behind the Government's foreign policy. He was, however, determined not to be drawn into war on any account. It seemed to me, viewing the proceedings from outside, that he was anxious to gather as much support as possible and use it to begin British rearmament on a modest scale.

*   *   *

The Conservative Party Conference was held at Bournemouth on the very day when Mussolini began his attack on Abyssinia and his bombs were falling on Adowa. In view of this, and not less of the now imminent general election, we all closed our ranks as party men.

I supported a resolution which was carried unanimously:

(1) To repair the serious deficiencies in the defence forces of the Crown, and, in particular, first, to organize our industry for speedy conversion to defence purposes, if need be.

(2) To make a renewed effort to establish equality in the air with the strongest foreign air force within striking distance of our shores.

(3) To rebuild the British Fleet and strengthen the Royal Navy, so as to safeguard our food and livelihood and preserve the coherence of the British Empire.

Hitherto in these years I had not desired office, having had so much of it, and being opposed to the Government on their Indian policy. But with the passage of the India Bill, which was to take some years to come into force, this barrier had fallen away. The growing German menace made me anxious to lay my hands upon our military machine. I could now feel very keenly what was coming. Distracted France and timid, peace-loving Britain would soon be confronted with the challenge of the European Dictators. I was in sympathy with the changing temper of the Labour Party. Here was the chance of a true National Government. It was understood that the Admiralty would be vacant, and I wished very much to go there should the Conservatives be returned to power. I was, of course, well aware that this desire was not shared by several of Mr. Baldwin's principal colleagues. I represented a policy, and it was

known that I should strive for it whether from without or from within. If they could do without me, they would certainly be very glad. To some extent this depended upon their majority.

*   *   *

At the general election the Prime Minister spoke in strong terms of the need for rearmament, and his principal speech was devoted to the unsatisfactory condition of the Navy. However, having gained all that there was in sight upon a programme of sanctions and rearmament, he became very anxious to comfort the professional peace-loving elements in the nation, and allay any fears in their breasts which his talk about naval requirements might have caused. On October 1, two weeks before the poll, he made a speech to the Peace Society at the Guildhall. In the course of this he said, "I give you my word there will be no great armaments." In the light of the knowledge which the Government had of strenuous German preparations, this was a singular promise. Thus the votes both of those who sought to see the nation prepare itself against the dangers of the future, and of those who believed that peace could be preserved by praising its virtues, were gained.

*   *   *

I fought my contest in the Epping Division upon the need for rearmament and upon a severe and *bona-fide* policy of sanctions. Generally speaking I supported the Government, and although many of my Conservative friends had been offended by my almost ceaseless criticism of Government measures, I was returned by an ample majority. Upon the declaration of the poll I thought it right to safeguard my own position. "I take it from your vote, in view of the speeches I have made, that you desire me to exercise my independent judgment as a Member of Parliament, and in accordance with the highest traditions of that House, to give the fruits of my knowledge and experience freely and without fear." The result of the general election was a triumph for Mr. Baldwin. The electors accorded him a majority of two hundred and forty-seven over all other parties combined, and after five years of office he reached a position of personal power unequalled by any Prime Minister since the close of the Great War. All who had opposed him, whether on India or on the neglect of our defences, were stultified by this renewed vote of confidence, which he had gained by his skilful and fortunate tactics in home politics and by the esteem so widely felt for his personal character. Thus an administration more disastrous than any in our history saw all its errors and shortcomings acclaimed by the nation. There was, however, a bill to be paid, and it took the new House of Commons nearly ten years to pay it.

* * *

It had been widely bruited that I should join the Government as First Lord of the Admiralty. But after the figures of his victory had been proclaimed, Mr. Baldwin lost no time in announcing through the Central Office that there was no intention to include me in the Government. In this way he paid some of his debt to the pacifist deputation which he had received in the last days of the election. There was much mockery in the press about my exclusion. But now one can see how lucky I was. Over me beat the invisible wings.

And I had agreeable consolations. I set out with my paint-box for more genial climes without waiting for the meeting of Parliament.

* * *

There was an awkward sequel to Mr. Baldwin's triumph, for the sake of which we may sacrifice chronology. His Foreign Secretary, Sir Samuel Hoare, travelling through Paris to Switzerland on a well-earned skating holiday, had a talk with M. Laval, still French Foreign Minister. The result of this was the Hoare-Laval Pact of December 9. It is worth while to look a little into the background of this celebrated incident.

The idea of Britain leading the League of Nations against Mussolini's Fascist invasion of Abyssinia had carried the nation in one of its big swings. But once the election was over and the Ministers found themselves in possession of a majority which might give them for five years the guidance of the State, many tiresome consequences had to be considered. At the root of them all lay Mr. Baldwin's "There must be no war," and also, "There must be no large rearmament." This remarkable party manager, having won the election on world leadership against aggression, was profoundly convinced that we must keep peace at any price.

Moreover, now from the Foreign Office came a very powerful thrust. Sir Robert Vansittart never removed his eyes for one moment from the Hitler peril. He and I were of one mind on that point. And now British policy had forced Mussolini to change sides. Germany was no longer isolated. The four Western Powers were divided two against two instead of three against one. This marked deterioration in our affairs aggravated the anxiety in France. The French Government had already made the Franco-Italian agreement of January. Following thereupon had come the military convention with Italy. It was calculated that this convention saved eighteen French divisions from the Italian front for transference to the front against Germany. In his negotiations it is certain that M. Laval had given more than a hint to Mussolini that France would not trouble herself about anything that might happen to Abyssinia. The French had a considerable case to argue with British Ministers. First, for several years we had tried to make them reduce their army, which was all they had to live upon. Secondly, the British had had a very good run in the leadership of the League of Nations against Mussolini. They had even won an election upon it; and in democracies elections are very important. Thirdly, we had made a naval agreement, supposed to be very good for ourselves, which made us quite comfortable upon the seas apart from submarine warfare.

But what about the French front? How was it to be manned against the ever-growing German military power? Two divisions to be sent only under many reservations was all the British could offer for the first six months; so really they should not talk too much. Now the British Government, in a fine flow of martial, moral and world sentiment, "fifty nations led by one," were making a mortal feud with Italy. France had much to worry about, and only very silly people, of whom there are extremely large numbers in every country, could ignore all this. If Britain had used her naval power, closed the Suez Canal, and defeated the Italian Navy in a general engagement, she would have had the right to call the tune in Europe. But on the contrary, she had definitely declared that whatever happened she would not go to war over Abyssinia. Honest Mr. Baldwin; a triumphant vote in the constituencies; a solid Tory majority for five more years; every aspect of righteous indignation, but no war, no war! The French, therefore, felt very strongly that they should not be drawn into permanent estrangement from Italy because of all the strong feeling which had suddenly surged up in England against Mussolini. Especially did they feel this when they remembered that Britain had bowed before the Italian naval challenge in the Mediterranean, and when two divisions of troops were all we could send at the outset to help France if she were invaded by Germany. One can certainly understand Monsieur Laval's point of view at this time.

Now in December a new set of arguments marched upon the scene. Mussolini, hard pressed by sanctions, and under the very heavy threat of "fifty nations led by one," would, it was whispered, welcome a compromise on Abyssinia. Poison gas, though effective against the native Ethiopians, would certainly not elevate the name of Italy in the world. The Abyssinians were being defeated. They were not, it was said, prepared to make large concessions and wide surrenders of territory. Could not a peace be made which gave Italy what she had aggressively demanded and left Abyssinia four-fifths of her entire empire? Vansittart, who happened to be in Paris at the time the Foreign Secretary passed through, and was thus drawn into the affair, should not be misjudged because he thought continuously of the German threat, and wished to have Britain and France organised at their strongest to face this major danger, with Italy in their rear a friend and not a foe.

But the British nation from time to time gives way to waves of crusading sentiment. More than any other country in the world, it is at rare intervals ready to fight for a cause or a theme, just because it is convinced in its heart and soul that it will not get any material advantage out of the conflict. Baldwin and his Ministers had given a great uplift to Britain in their resistance to Mussolini at Geneva. They had gone so far that their only salvation before history was to go all lengths. Unless they were prepared to back words and gestures by action, it might have been better to keep out of it all, like the United States, and let things rip and see what happened. Here was an arguable plan. But it was not the plan they had adopted. They had appealed to the millions, and the unarmed, and hitherto unconcerned, millions had answered with a loud shout, overpowering all other cries, "Yes, we will march against evil, and we will march now. Give us the weapons."

The new House of Commons was a spirited body. With all that lay before them in the next ten years, they had need to be. It was therefore with a horrible shock that, while tingling from the election, they received the news that a compromise had been made between Sir Samuel Hoare and M. Laval about Abyssinia. This crisis nearly cost Mr. Baldwin his political life. It shook Parliament and the nation to its base. Mr. Baldwin fell almost overnight from his pinnacle of acclaimed national leadership to a depth where he was derided and despised. His position in the House during these days was pitiful. He had never understood why people should worry about all these bothersome foreign affairs. They had a Conservative majority and no war. What more could they want? But the experienced pilot felt and measured the full force of the storm.

The Cabinet, on December 9, had approved the Hoare-Laval plan to partition Abyssinia between Italy and the Emperor. On the thirteenth the full text of the Hoare-Laval proposals was laid before the League. On the eighteenth the Cabinet abandoned the Hoare-Laval proposals, thus entailing the resignation of Sir Samuel Hoare. In the debate on the nineteenth Mr. Baldwin said:

I felt that these proposals went too far. I was not at all surprised at the expression of feeling in that direction. I was not expecting that deeper feeling that was manifest in many parts of the country on what I may call the grounds of conscience and of honour. The moment I am confronted with that, I know that something has happened that has appealed to the deepest feelings of our countrymen, that some note has been struck that brings back from them a response from the depths. I examined again all that I had done, and I felt that . . . there could not be support in this country behind those proposals even as terms of negotiation. It is perfectly obvious now that the proposals are absolutely and completely dead. This Government is certainly going to make no attempt to resurrect them. If there arose a storm when I knew I was in the right, I would let it break on me, and I would either survive it or break. If I felt after examination of myself that there was in that storm something which showed me that I had done something that was not wise or right, then I would bow to it.

The House accepted this apologia. The crisis passed. On his return from Geneva, Mr. Eden was summoned to 10 Downing Street by the Prime Minister to discuss the situation following Sir Samuel Hoare's resignation. Mr. Eden at once suggested that Sir Austen Chamberlain should be invited to take over the Foreign Office, and added that if desired he was prepared to serve under him in any capacity. Mr. Baldwin replied that he had already considered this and had informed Sir Austen himself that he did not feel able to offer the Foreign Office to him. This may have been due to Sir Austen's health. On December 22, Mr. Eden became Foreign Secretary. . . .

* * *

The collapse of Abyssinian resistance and the annexation of the whole country by Italy produced unhelpful effects in German public opinion. Even those elements which did not approve of Mussolini's policy or action admired the swift, efficient, and ruthless manner in which, as it seemed, the campaign had been conducted. The general view was that Great Britain had emerged thoroughly weakened. She had earned the undying hatred of Italy; she had wrecked the Stresa Front once and for all; and her loss of prestige in the world contrasted agreeably with the growing strength and repute of the new Germany. "I am impressed," wrote one of our representatives in Bavaria, "by the note of contempt in references to Great Britain in many quarters. . . . It is to be feared that Germany's attitude in the negotiations for a settlement in Western Europe and for a more general settlement of European and extra-European questions will be found to have stiffened." An article in the *Muenchener Zeitung* (May 16, 1936) contains some illuminating passages:

The English like a comfortable life compared with our German standards. This does not indeed mean that they are incapable of sustained efforts, but they avoid them so far as they can, without impairing their personal and national security. They also control means and wealth which have enabled them, in contrast with us, for a century or so, to increase their capital more or less automatically. . . . After the war, in which the English after some preliminary hesitation showed certainly an amazing energy, the British masters of the world thought they had at last earned a little rest. They disarmed along the whole line — in civil life even more than on land and sea. They reconciled themselves to abandoning the two-power [naval] standard and accepted parity with America. . . . How about the Army? How about the air force? . . . For the land and air defence forces England needs above all men, not merely money, but also the lives of her citizens for Empire defence. Indeed, of the eleven thousand men needed for the new air programme, seven thousand are lacking. Again, the small Regular Army shows a large deficiency, about one whole division, and the Territorial Army (a sort of Sunday-School for amateur soldiers) is so far below its authorised numbers that it cannot in any way be considered an effective combatant force. Mr. Baldwin himself said a short time ago that he had no intention of changing the system of recruiting by the introduction of conscription.

A policy which seeks to achieve success by postponing decisions can today hardly hope to resist the whirlwind which is shaking Europe and indeed the whole world. Few are the men who, upon national and not upon party grounds, rage against the spinelessness and ambiguous attitude of the Government, and hold them responsible for the dangers into which the Empire is being driven all unaware. The masses seem to agree with the Government that the situation will improve by marking time, and that by means of small adjustments and carefully thought-out manœuvres the balance can once against be rectified. . . .

Today all Abyssinia is irrevocably, fully, and finally Italian alone. This being so, neither Geneva nor London can have any doubt that only the use of extraordinary force can drive the Italians out of Abyssinia. But neither the power nor the courage to use force is at hand.

All this was only too true. His Majesty's Government had imprudently advanced to champion a great world cause. They had led fifty nations forward with much brave language. Confronted with brute facts Mr. Baldwin had recoiled. Their policy had for a long time been designed to give satisfaction to powerful elements of opinion at home rather than to seek the realities of the European situation. By estranging Italy they had upset the whole balance of Europe and gained nothing for Abyssinia. They had led the League of Nations into an utter fiasco, most damaging if not fatally injurious to its effective life as an institution.

PRELUDE TO WORLD WAR II

GAETANO SALVEMINI

The liberal political convictions of Gaetano Salvemini (1873–1957) caused him to leave Italy in the nineteen-twenties rather than to compromise in any way with the established fascist regime. After an extended sojourn in Great Britain, he came to the United States in 1932 where he was long a stimulating and impressive figure at Harvard University. Professor Salvemini was the author of numerous historical works, many of them biting attacks on Mussolini. Freely acknowledging his bias, averse to directing responsibility to "corporate" abstractions as Italy or the State, he painstakingly collected evidence to develop the liability of definite persons. His indictment knew no national boundaries; regarding Britain as the fatherland of lovers of freedom the world over, his opinion of the intelligence and integrity of the men who then governed was dealt a body blow.

IN November 1925, while on a Mediterranean cruise in his private yacht, Sir Austen Chamberlain [British Foreign Secretary] stopped at Rapallo and renewed the ties with Mussolini established earlier in Rome. "All my pleasant impressions of him gained in Rome," wrote Sir Austen, "were renewed and confirmed." His host was "the simplest and sincerest of men when he was not posing as the dictator."

It is not part of my business as Foreign Secretary to appreciate his action in the domestic policies of Italy, but if I ever had to choose in my own country between anarchy and dictatorship, I expect I should be on the side of the dictator. . . . I believe him to be accused of crimes *in which he had no share,* and I suspect him to have connived *unwillingly* at other outrages he would have prevented *if he could.* But I am confident that he is a patriot and a sincere man; I trust his word when given, and I think we might easily go far before finding an Italian with whom it would be as easy for the British Government to work. . . .

[While in this frame of mind Chamberlain and Mussolini came to an agreement concerning Ethiopia.] This country was bounded to the north, east, and south by the possessions of Italy, France, and Great Britain, which cut it off from the sea. In the Treaty of December 14, 1906, the three surrounding Powers agreed not to "infringe in any way on the sovereign rights" of the Emperor of Ethiopia, but at the same time they divided that country into three spheres of influence. The eastern territories, or the Lake Tana region, which border Sudan, went to Great Britain; Italy was assigned the central territories between Addis Ababa and the Lake Tana zone; and the eastern part, from Addis Ababa to French Somaliland, was allotted to France. In addition, they pledged not to undertake the building of any railway or to initiate any other form of economic penetration without previously coming to a three-way agreement. Nothing much was said or done about these matters for many years because the three European countries had other problems to cope with,

From Gaetano Salvemini, *Prelude to World War II* (New York, 1954), pp. 72, 74–75, 191–194, 210–211, 223–225, 294–299, 325–329, 365–366, 395–399. Reprinted by permission of Doubleday and Company, Inc. and Victor Gollancz, Ltd.

and because Ethiopia was for a long time rent by domestic struggles not propitious to foreign economic penetration. . . .

Around 1922, Emperor Haile Selassie (then Regent Diazmach Tafari) had restored a degree of order in the country. In September 1923, he secured Ethiopia's admission to the League of Nations, subject to reservations regarding slavery and arms traffic. His application was sponsored by the French and Italian Governments. The British Government objected on the ground that neither domestic slavery nor slave traffic had as yet been abolished in Ethiopia. But the French Government was then at loggerheads with the British over the Ruhr, while Mussolini was on good terms with Paris and on bad terms with London because of Corfu. The British Foreign Office, confronted with joint Franco-Italian action, gave way, and Ethiopia was therefore admitted to the League. In 1924, Ethiopia's Regent took a trip to Europe to establish regular relations with the countries of "superior civilization." He was officially received at Rome during the very days in the summer of 1924 when the Fascist régime was rocked to its foundations by the Matteotti scandal and the body of the murdered man was being sought without success. A comic sheet in Rome represented, regardless of the truth, the illustrious scion of King Solomon and the Queen of Sheba under the guise of a black cannibal, whispering to the Italian Chief of Police: "You can tell me in all confidence; did you eat him?" His Ethiopian Highness must have felt scant admiration for Fascist "superior civilization."

Now that the Regent of Ethiopia, thanks to French and Italian sponsorship, had been allowed to affix his signature to the Covenant of the League of Nations, which stipulated that all partners should guarantee the full independence and territorial integrity of the co-signatories, the British and Italian Governments, on December 16 and 20, 1925, exchanged notes by which the British Government pledged itself to support the Italian Government in its endeavour to obtain the concession to build the railway from Eritrea to Italian Somaliland; moreover, it would raise no obstacle to the efforts of the Italian Government to secure from the French Government the abandonment to Italian influence of the French sphere lying between the French Colony of Djibuti and Addis Ababa. In return, the Italian Government bound itself to support the British Government in its endeavour to obtain from the Ethiopian Government the concession to build the dam on Lake Tana and a motor road extending from Sudan to the Lake. The agreement provided that should only one of the two signatories be granted the desired concessions, the successful signatory would not "relax his wholehearted efforts to secure a corresponding satisfaction for the other Government concerned." It is interesting to note that Mussolini (or his "experts") were still thinking, at the end of 1925, in terms of nineteenth-century railways; they had not yet realized that railways had been superseded by motor-roads.

This agreement in appearance was of an economic nature, and did not explicitly allow Mussolini to wage war on Ethiopia whenever he saw fit. But Mussolini could not have built and operated a railway cutting across the whole of Ethiopia from north to south had he not been entitled to establish military control over that territory. What Sir Austen was actually doing in December 1925 was to pledge the British Foreign Office not to interfere with Mussolini even if he landed himself in a war with Ethiopia, on condition that British "special interests" in the Tana region remained unchallenged. . . .

SILENCE AT STRESA

At the Stresa Conference (April 11–14), the Ethiopian question was never officially discussed. It is obvious that "silence in the face of undisguised Italian preparation for war" was bound to be interpreted by Mussolini "to mean that Great Britain, like France, was content to regard the African adventure with benevolent eyes."

Sir Charles Petrie writes that at Stresa, "for some reason *which has not been satisfactorily explained*, no mention of Abyssinia was made, with the result that the Duce drew the not-unnatural inference that Great Britain was not interested." As a matter of fact, the explanation is there and wholly satisfactory: the written Chamberlain-Mussolini agreement of December 1925, and the verbal Laval-Mussolini agreement of January 10, 1935. Nobody explicitly approved of what everybody knew Mussolini was planning. All abstained from embarrassing him. *"On s'est abstenu de le gêner,"* Laval was reported to have said. But omission may carry the same responsibility as commission.

A few months later, Sir Samuel Hoare, who in June had succeeded Sir John Simon as Foreign Secretary, was asked in the House of Commons (I.vii.35) whether there was any basis for the "rumour" that "at Stresa" assurances had been given to Mussolini on behalf of France that Italy would have a free hand in Abyssinia so far as France was concerned, and that the British delegates were aware of these assurances and had said nothing with regard to them, thus giving passive assent to a policy of that kind. Sir Samuel Hoare answered that there was "no foundation whatever" for the report that "at Stresa" "the British Government and the French Government had given some kind of undertaking to the Italian Government under which they were supposed to be prepared to give the Italian Government a free hand in Abyssinia." He added that "the question of Abyssinia was never discussed between *the delegates* of the three Governments *at Stresa*." As for France, "it was for the French Government to make the answer." None the less, "he felt quite certain that the French Government had given no undertaking *either at Stresa or in any other conversations* that would justify any settlement of that kind." He was equally certain that the French Government "had taken no action that would be contrary to its obligations either under the Covenant or under the existing treaties."

The reader should notice that Sir Samuel left to the French the task of contradicting "rumours" in which they and not the English were concerned. As for what had happened at Stresa, the British Foreign Minister said that no undertaking had been given *at Stresa* in April 1935. He did not say that no undertaking had been given by Laval *at Rome* in January 1935, or by Sir Austen Chamberlain *at Rapallo* in December 1925.

According to Sir Samuel, the Ethiopian question was never discussed at Stresa by *the delegates*. When the matter again came before the House of Commons on October 22, 1935, Sir Samuel admitted that the Abyssinian question had been discussed at Stresa between "members of the two delegations." On the following day, Lloyd George asked:

What delegations? The only man that mattered in the Italian delegation was Signor Mussolini. Were there any conversations between the only members of the delegation that mattered? . . . What was the use of delegating this discussion to experts and clerks who had no authority? Who took part in those discussions? . . . We ought to know.

Eden, speaking after Lloyd George, endeavoured to evade this issue, but Lloyd George insisted: "There was no discussion between our Prime Minister and our Foreign Secretary and Signor Mussolini?" Eden answered: "No *official* discussion at all." Lloyd George again insisted: "Were there *any discussions?*" Eden: "Not *between the heads of delegation.*"

Among the British officials at Stresa there were Sir Robert Vansittart (later Lord Vansittart), Permanent Under-Secretary to the Foreign Office, and the expert in East African affairs, Sir Maurice Peterson. The Liberal M.P., Sir Archibald Sinclair, pointed out in the House of Commons (June 23, 1936) that the British delegation had had their expert on Abyssinian affairs with them at Stresa:

They never once dared to call him into the room with Signor Mussolini in order to discuss these matters. What should have been done at Stresa was to face Mussolini with the declaration: "If you go on with your Abyssinian policy, you will find that the whole might of Britain will be ranged on the side of the League in order to assert its authority against the aggressor."

Lord Vansittart states that at Stresa he "warned" the Italians in "personal talks" about the Ethiopian muddle. He does not elucidate, however, as to the exact tenor of his warnings. Did he merely inform them that an Italo-Ethiopian war would be extremely unpopular in England, and did he stop there? Or did he add that the British Government would be forced by the pressure of public opinion to take sides with the League of Nations against Italy? While evading this point, Lord Vansittart explains his tactics on the following grounds: (1) Mussolini would not have heeded a warning from England alone, once Laval "had taken care" of the business; and (2) "it seemed better tactics, while keeping an eye on Laval, first to secure agreement on Austria, that is to provide a bait before administering a monition." These words mean nothing. Laval and Mussolini had already reached an accord on the Austria question in January 1935, and they did not need any inducement on that score, unless Lord Vansittart offered active British support against any attempt by Hitler at Anschluss: but this support was never promised: "It was notorious," writes Lord Vansittart, "that Britain still had a horror of 'commitments.'" If the British had a terror of commitments, there could be at Stresa neither bribes nor monitions.

According to the diplomatic documents used by Villari, the Ethiopian affair was not discussed by the protagonists at Stresa, but "there were more or less private conversations between certain officials of the British and Italian delegations." The Italians explained that Italy was obliged "to guarantee the security of her colonies" and also to forestall the increase of German influence even in Ethiopia. The British officials were of the opinion that "vigorous action was inopportune, in view of the European situation at the moment; an undertaking of that nature would have had repercussions on Italy's political situation and military strength in Europe; colonial expeditions could very well be long-drawn-out and require a great outlay of military and financial effort." The Italians were informed that "a committee of experts had begun the study of British interests in Ethiopia." It would appear from this source too, therefore, that the British Government failed to make an outright statement of its intentions to honour its obligations under the Covenant of the League should Mussolini's venture result in war.

In an interview with the *Morning Post* of September 17, 1935, Mussolini stated — and nobody ever contradicted him on this score — that after the Stresa Conference he once again instructed his Ambassador in London, on May 1, to invite the British Government to open friendly talks with the Italian Government on the Ethiopian question. "Even that overture led to inconclusive conversations." The British Foreign Office did not need conclusions. The conclusion had already been agreed upon by Sir Austen Chamberlain in December 1925.

Mussolini revealed in the same interview that the words "of Europe" had been inserted by him in the official communiqué "to show that the African situation had been omitted." Then the whole of his Cabinet came in (September 28, 1935), and stated that the British Government, from January 29 onwards, had been informed "in the most loyal manner of the colonial objectives of Italian policy," and that Italian interests had been "recognized in bilateral agreements by Great Britain herself." This was a clear-cut reference to the Chamberlain-Mussolini agreement of December 1925.

The British Foreign Office ignored the

hint at the agreement of 1925, but protested that the reference to Great Britain's attitude was "completely misleading." Sir Eric Drummond had expressed to the Italian Government, on February 28, Great Britain's serious concern at the general situation and had informed them of the reactions of public opinion in England against a war-like attitude on the part of Italy; this was again repeated to Signor Grandi in London by Sir Robert Vansittart on April 17, and by the British delegation at Geneva on April 30; further warnings had been given on May 3 and 22. The British had always stressed their obligations under the Covenant:

Although the question did not come up officially at Stresa, it formed the subject of conversations between officials, and a very serious warning of the consequences of military action in Abyssinia was given through officials.

The British Foreign Office was careful not to make clear the only point which was pertinent: Mussolini did not need to be warned about the general situation or public opinion, or even the existence of the Covenant; he should have been told squarely that the British Government intended to carry out the Covenant, and not to stultify it. If Lord Vansittart and Sir Maurice Peterson had warned the Italians that the British Foreign Office would oppose Mussolini's adventure, this fact would have been made clear by the "British quarters" in September 1935. . . .

In the Far Eastern crisis of 1931 and following years, Japan and China, owing to their great distance from Europe might as well have been on the moon. If a man sees a cat crushed under a car, he loses his appetite; yet the same man can calmly eat his breakfast while reading in his morning paper that thousands of men, women, and children have been engulfed in some cataclysmic earthquake. The Japanese Government and its accessories in Europe could count on the ignorance of people too preoccupied with difficulties at home to be concerned with events in remote lands. People's minds in both America and Europe were distraught with the economic depression that had started in 1929 and was at its worst in 1931–2. Moreover, the Japanese went about their business quietly, so as to attract the least possible attention. Last but not least, Russia and the United States were equally if not more interested in the Sino-Japanese affair than Britain and France. Neither Russia nor the United States was a member of the League of Nations. Soviet Russia had taken an ambiguous stand, most likely because of her military weakness in the Far East. As for the United States, Sir John Simon had maintained that he could not count on the United States for a policy other than the one he was pursuing. A handful of specialists alone realized the gravity of what was happening.

The situation was quite different during the crisis of 1935. Italy lies in the middle of the Mediterranean, and is in direct contact with the whole of Western, Central, and South-eastern Europe. "Since Ethiopia lay in the heart of another continent, three thousand miles from Italy, and Italian troops en route to East Africa had to pass through the Suez Canal, Mussolini carried out his rehearsals in a theatre with all seats filled and the curtain rolled up." Not only could Italy not be ignored, but Mussolini made the greatest possible hullaballoo in order not to be ignored. One must do him the justice of admitting that he spared neither speeches nor interviews to acquaint the world with his intention of attacking Ethiopia. Never previously in history has any war been clamorously announced for nine months beforehand. Mussolini supplied historians with this innovation in diplomatic technique. He hoped to cow the Ethiopians into submission by a display of overwhelming strength and heroic willpower. At the same time he had to stir up the Italians.

He completely failed to frighten the Ethiopians. Remembering that they had annihilated an Italian army at Adowa forty years earlier, they still believed themselves invulnerable behind their natural defences. They were sure they could stop modern tanks and planes with their primitive weapons. Even if he had been able to reach a compromise with Mussolini, Haile Selassie could not have carried it out in a feudal country where many of the local chieftains were ready to seize upon any pretext to rebel and overthrow him.

As for Italy, Mussolini had not succeeded, even as late as the summer of 1935, in rousing the mass of the population from the depths of an apathy induced by the abuses of "propaganda" and nine years of economic crisis.

On the other hand, he raised a storm in England. The poll, initiated when no one foresaw an Italo-Ethiopian war, became, during the first half of 1935, a demonstration of hostility against Mussolini's policy. A clash developed between Mussolini and the British public — that is, those Liberals, Labourites and, in general, those men and women who had opposed their Government during the Boer War, forty years earlier, and who had swept Lloyd George out of office in 1922 when he had tried to go to war with Turkey.

In 1935, the British Conservative leaders were in the hapless position of being answerable to a people who were accustomed to having some say in the policies of their Government. Had they looked the other way while Mussolini was attacking Ethiopia, the Conservatives would have lost heavily in the general elections due in the following autumn. Moreover, if the London Cabinet had ignored what was happening in East Africa, the small Powers would have been made aware that they could expect no protection against the eventual aggression of a great Power. A revolt of their delegates might have broken out in the Assembly of the League. Such a revolt might have brought about a landslide in favour of the Labour Party in the forthcoming elections.

It was necessary, therefore, not to run counter to the British people's faith in the League of Nations, while implementing at one and the same time the Chamberlain-Mussolini agreement of 1925. The British Government had to go through the motions of siding with the British people against Mussolini, while never having the slightest intention of opposing him. . . .

CONSEQUENCES OF THE ANGLO-GERMAN NAVAL ACCORD

Laval read the news of the Anglo-German Naval Treaty in the papers, and immediately protested to the English Ambassador. A Franco-Italian military convention, which had been drawn up during the preceding months, was immediately (June 19) signed by General Gamelin, Commander-in-Chief of the French forces, and General Badoglio, Chief of the General Staff in Italy. In the event of a German move against Austria, a French army would be sent to Italy, to join with Italian and Yugoslav forces in a march on Vienna, and effect a junction with the Czech forces. At the same time an Italian army should be sent to France to operate between Belfort and the Swiss border, side by side with French units. The air forces of the two countries would join against southern Germany. The Italian Military Intelligence Service (SIM) suspended its activities in France and made arrangements to work hand in glove with the French Counter-Espionage Office (2me Bureau) against Germany.

Mussolini's stock soared to new heights on the Paris political market. People felt that in the light of the Anglo-German agreement, the Laval-Mussolini entente, even if at Ethiopia's expense, was more reasonable than ever. The *Intransigeant* — a paper intransigently loyal to Mussolini — found in the Anglo-German agreement a reason to approve of Italy's "work of civilization" in Ethiopia and to warn Britain that France would stand by her Latin sister (June 19). Even a man like Pertinax wrote: "Nothing is now left of the Franco-British co-operation announced in February and reinforced by Italy at Stresa. Therefore let us have no intervention in the Italo-Abyssinian controversy."

In addition, Laval decided to try to come to an agreement with Hitler before the British Foreign Office forestalled him. To help him in this effort there was a large current of opinion available in France. Now that Stalin had advised the French Communists to turn ultra-patriotic overnight, the French monarchists, clericals, and Fascists were seized with panic lest the "Bolshevists" get the upper hand in French internal affairs. Blinded by their terror, they adopted the plan of coming to terms not only with Mussolini, but also with Hitler. Laval adopted their line of thought.

But how could any negotiations for an entente with Hitler be successful so long as the Franco-Russian treaty of alliance existed?

In his memorandum of October 2, 1945, written in the prison of Fresnes, Laval explained his action as follows:

I wanted our country to live on terms of good neighbourhood with Germany. I publicly advocated a *rapprochement* and an entente in 1931, and relations of good neighbourhood in 1935. But at the same time, because I was aware of Hitler's boundless ambition and the ever-growing power of his armies, because I knew he wanted to build the Great Reich and insure German hegemony over Europe, I carried out a virtual encirclement of Germany. It is to that end that I signed the Rome agreements with Mussolini. It is for that reason that I facilitated the reconciliation of Italy with Yugoslavia, and I induced Austria to accept military aid from Czechoslovakia, Yugoslavia, and Rumania for her defence. It is to that end that I negotiated and signed the Franco-Soviet pact.

This is not the whole story. Laval does not explain why, after signing the Franco-Soviet pact, he failed to have it ratified by Parliament, and why journalists friendly to him poked fun at it. There is only one explanation for this double-dealing. He thought he might postpone ratification of the treaty, meanwhile passing the word to his followers and friends to campaign against the U.S.S.R. and the not-yet-ratified treaty of alliance. This treaty was to be not a definite and permanent instrument through which French security against German attack might be ensured, but a provisional shelter to be made use of while negotiating the agreement with Hitler. When that agreement had been reached, the Russian treaty, not yet ratified, would be put aside and forgotten; Stalin would be left in the lurch. Of course, one of the provisos of the Franco-German agreement would give Hitler a free hand in Eastern Europe, in the same way as the Laval-Mussolini agreement had given the latter a free hand in Ethiopia. If war could not be avoided, it should be localized in Eastern Europe. In view of this manœuvre, the Franco-Soviet Pact had to be left dangling in mid-air. "It looked as if he had come to terms with Russia only to be able to make a better bargain with the Fuehrer." He repeated to his confidants: "I signed the pact but it will not be ratified quickly. By then I shall have reached an understanding with the Reich." He was wont to reiterate that "he needed the friendship of Italy to reach an understanding with the Germans. And to achieve peace in Europe and the world an understanding with Germany was indispensable."

Another point which Laval glossed over in his Fresnes memorandum concerns Franco-British relations. Hitler's agreement with France at Russia's expense would have made France less dependent on England. This was precisely the danger point which gave British diplomats cause for worry. This was why they tried to forestall Laval in making friends with Hitler. Thus, each hoping to outsmart his neighbour, London and Paris paved the way for the coming cataclysm.

Lord Vansittart tells us that "there were suspicions that he [Laval] was in German pay. . . . During the period which I am about to describe [1935], Laval actually asked Hitler to help him in retaining power. . . . Money did not run big in French politics, and Laval made more than was normally explicable." With less self-righteousness, Lord Vansittart might have remarked that in view of the fact that the British Foreign Office always wavered between a Germany judged to be the weaker and a France judged to be the stronger, it was inevitable that not only Laval but many other French politicians should be tempted to escape from insecure British help through a direct entente with Hitler, and this without being bribed with German money. British blindness was sufficient to achieve that, though German money may also have played its part.

Money or no money, Laval was too crafty. His craftiness discredited him in Britain and Russia, and in Germany, too. Who could rely upon such a man?

But there were people in London, Berlin, and Moscow who were craftier than he. He made the fundamental mistake of never understanding that it would be impossible for France to guarantee Austria, Czechoslovakia, and Poland against Hitler, if Stalin, left out in the cold, joined hands with Hitler. The British Conservatives were more logical than he in abandoning to Hitler not only Russia, but the whole of Eastern Europe. . . .

THE LEAGUE OF NATIONS IN ACTION

The General Assembly of the League met on September 9. While it was spending two days on matters of procedure, an exchange of views took place between Laval, Hoare, Eden, and Lord Vansittart on September 10. Its outcome was revealed by Laval in the French Chamber of Deputies, on December 28, 1935:

On September 10 I had some conversations at Geneva with Sir Samuel Hoare and Mr. Eden. . . . We discussed and examined—in that spirit of close co-operation which ought always to animate French and British statesmen — the grave situation with which the world was going to be confronted by the Italo-Ethiopian war. We found ourselves instantaneously in agreement upon ruling out military sanctions, not adopting any measure of naval blockade, never contemplating the closure of the Suez Canal — in a word, we agreed to rule out everything that might lead to war. We then examined what sanctions of a financial or economic nature might be adopted by us. I have no recollection of there being the slightest difficulty between the British ministers and myself. . . . We were in aggreement that such measures as financial sanctions or the embargo on arms should first be submitted to a committee which had not yet been set up, and then that other measures might be adopted, notably the refusal to buy from or sell to Italy.

As was natural, nobody in Geneva knew anything about the agreement of September 10. Thus, the stage was set for the great humbug of the following days.

On that very day (September 10), the French Ambassador in London was asking the Foreign Office "for information as to the extent to which the French Government might be assured in the future of the immediate and effective application by the United Kingdom of all the sanctions provided in Article 16 of the Covenant, in the event of a violation of the Covenant and a resort to force *in Europe*." A question of this nature, coming just as Hoare, Eden, and Laval were agreeing at Geneva not to apply either "immediate" or "effective" sanctions, was ill-timed in the extreme. There can be only one explanation. The French Ambassador had been instructed to take that step before Laval left for Geneva, when the latter did not expect Hoare and Eden to consent to reducing sanctions to a farce. The London move was most likely devised in the belief that the Ambassador would receive an unsatisfactory answer, and this would permit Laval to inform Hoare and Eden at Geneva that he could not commit himself to a policy that was valid for Africa and not for Europe. The immediate consent of Hoare and Eden to the farce of "partial" sanctions put an end to further discussion. But that word "Europe" remained as the crux of the question.

After settling the matter of sanctions with Laval, Sir Samuel Hoare came before the Assembly of the League (September 11), and delivered [his famous promise that Britain would support the League]. . . . He took good care to warn his audience that "if the burden is to be borne, it must be borne collectively; if risks for peace are to be run, they must be run by all; the security of the many cannot be ensured solely by the effort of a few, however powerful they may be." But nobody would have quarrelled with him on this point, inasmuch as he also stated that His Majesty's Government would "be second to none in its intention to fulfil, within the measure of its capacity, the obligation which the Covenant laid upon it. . . ."

If the secret agreement of September 10 had been known, Sir Samuel's public speech of September 11 before the Assembly of the League would have been greeted with a tempest of boos and hisses. On the contrary, it met with an immense ovation. For five days — from the 11th to the 14th of September — the delegates of almost all the Governments represented in the Assembly came forward to support the British point of view and to promise their co-operation. The representatives of Australia, India, South Africa, Canada, and New Zealand all signified their full adherence to the position taken by Sir Samuel Hoare.

Litvinov also contributed to the grand parade:

For the Soviet delegation there is only the question of defending the Covenant of the League as an instrument of peace. . . . We may need it more than once, and probably on still more serious occasions. . . . The State I represent will be second to none in the loyal discharge of its international obligations. . . .

Then Laval came in:

Sir Samuel Hoare has told us of the determination of Great Britain to adhere *without reservation* to the system of collective security. . . . No country has received with greater satisfaction than France the words of the British Foreign Secretary. . . . I rejoice with my country, for my country fully understands all the need for a close collaboration with Great Britain for the defence of peace and the safeguarding *of Europe*. . . . The solidarity *in the responsibilities of all kinds in all circumstances of time and place* which is implied for the future by such a declaration constitutes a date in the history of the League of Nations. . . . France is loyal to the Covenant. . . . The Covenant is our international law. . . . Our obligations are inscribed in the Covenant. France will not evade them.

At the same time Laval made it clear that France, on January 7, 1935, had reached a final settlement of all her differences with Italy: he had left nothing undone "to prevent any blow to the new policy happily established between France and Italy"; and Mussolini "was prepared to persevere in this collaboration." As for the Italo-Ethiopian dispute, the task of conciliation, though doubtless a difficult one, was not hopeless. There was no disagreement between France and Great Britain. Both wanted a solution that met Italy's legitimate desires while respecting the sovereignty of Ethiopia. All loop-holes through which relevant issues might be evaded were left wide open.

While the grand parade was in full swing in Geneva, Laval continued to discuss with Eden (who had to keep an eye on the imminent British election) whether it might not be advisable to avoid the Italo-Ethiopian war by setting up in Ethiopia a régime similar to that of Egypt. Once the parade was over, he discussed with the Italian ambassador whether the problem could not be solved by conferring upon Italy a mandate over Ethiopia. Even Avenol, Secretary-General of the League of Nations, explained to Aloisi [the Italian delegate] that in the discussion which would arise out of the work done by the Committee of Five it would be unwise to stress that Ethiopia's peripheral provinces had been annexed to the central nucleus by conquest. This had happened before Ethiopia had been accepted as a member of the League of Nations; thus she had acquired the right to have her territorial integrity respected, whatever its origins. But the question of slavery and of the treatment meted out by the central Government to conquered populations offered a good platform for discussion. By asserting the need to solve these problems in accordance with the provisions of the Covenant, Mussolini could obtain improvements on the August proposals. The mission of helping Ethiopia might be entrusted more explicitly than in those proposals to the three signatory Powers of the Treaty of 1906, it being understood that London and Paris would in practice give Italy a free hand. The Chairman of the Committee of Five, the Spanish delegate Madariaga, also proposed that the reorganization of the Ethiopian Army be turned over to Italy.

It is highly improbable that Mussolini was not informed by Laval about the agreement of September 10. Laval told the Chamber of Deputies on December 28, 1935: "Italy has always been informed of our intentions and engagements, and I have never gone back on any of our pledges." The correspondent of the *Manchester Guardian* sent out the following dispatch from Geneva on September 13:

I am able to say that M. Laval has now definitely pledged the French Government to participate in economic and financial sanctions, but not in military or naval sanctions, in which he includes the closing of the Suez Canal to Italian ships, and to the ships of any nation carrying Italian soldiers or war material or supplies for the Italian army. . . . M. Laval has, I understand, given an undertaking to Mussolini that France will not join in any but economic and financial sanctions, so long as he (M. Laval) is Prime Minister, and Signor Mussolini has said that he would not regard French participation only in economic and financial sanctions as an unfriendly act.

Augur, also, cabled the *New York Times* (15.ix) that it had been decided that sanctions should be "non-belligerent": "in other words, the pressure to be applied shall be economic." A few days later, he foresaw that Mussolini would quieten down "upon assurance that sanctions would be neither military nor of a nature seriously to imperil the standard of living of the Italian populace" (*NYT*. 19.ix). The London *Daily Telegraph*, too, informed its readers that in his conversation with Laval, Aloisi had urged upon him the extreme importance of pressing Britain to abstain from adopting any major sanctions which would make general war inevitable.

Baron Aloisi apparently implied that economic sanctions, of a relatively mild character, would not be regarded in Rome as a challenge which need necessarily to be regarded as an unfriendly act involving recourse to war (19.ix).

Thus Mussolini arrogated unto himself the right to dictate what sanctions might or might not be applied. Laval, Hoare, and Eden decided to adopt sanctions, but they would not take any action if, in the opinion of Mussolini, it led to war. . . .

The Committee that, in line with the decision taken in April 1935, was to define the measures to be applied against an aggressor under Article 16 of the Covenant was set up, after due procrastination, at the end of May. As was to be expected, it begat two sub-committees, which issued two reports in August. They recommended that sanctions should not inflict unnecessary hardships on the innocent citizens of the treaty-breaking country. Food supplies essential to the subsistence of civilian populations should therefore not be withheld. Sanctions should have as their sole object the obstruction of war effort. The most obvious step in that direction was the withholding of arms and munitions, and of key products and raw materials essential to the armament industry. But the raw materials might be essential to ordinary industrial life, and inasmuch as it would be difficult to determine to what ultimate use they might be put, and inasmuch as no hardship was to be imposed upon any single individual, how could raw materials vital to the armament industry be listed? Exports from the law-breaking country to other countries might be interrupted, and since exports pay for imports, the embargo on exports would be equivalent to the cutting off of essential imports. In this case, other countries would suffer no less than the treaty-breaking country. Thus, this method also must be avoided on humanitarian grounds. Credit facilities might be withheld. But unscrupulous intermediaries might help the guilty country to circumvent this restriction. Moreover, the use of economic and financial sanctions might be almost as damaging to the economic life of the other countries. In addition, unless all nations were willing to enforce sanctions, non-participating countries could supply all the needs of the repudiating country. The non-participation of a single important producer might easily nullify all measures, unless vast international machinery were set up to supervise exporters, merchants, and shipowners. Implicit conclusion: take no action. The Committee and its sub-committees obviously thought that their task was to act as some sort of Animal Rescue League, rather than to devise means of preventing or stopping war. By concentrating on the sufferings and misery of the civilian population in the aggressor country they forgot the greater sufferings and misery that would be inflicted on the fighting men and civilians of all the warring nations, more particularly in the territories where military operations would develop.

After receiving this report, the Committee, which should have listed the sanctions, instructed its chairman to appoint another sub-committee to investigate the question of key-products needed for the manufacture of arms; their work was to be completed by November 30. This plethora of committees was not meant to discourage Mussolini.

After war had started in East Africa, the time to put sanctions into effect arrived. But in France the pacifist movement had played havoc with common sense. At a meeting of the Confédération Générale du Travail, held in Paris on September 23, the Secretary-General of the Confédération, Jouhaux, stated that "while French workers urged their Government to remain faithful to the League Covenant in order to maintain peace . . . they did not agree with their British comrades in demanding military sanctions." He was cheered. Other trade union leaders spoke against military sanctions and ended their speeches by shouting, "We not only hate war, we hate all wars." They, too, were given an ovation. The correspondent of the *Manchester Guardian* (I.x) reported that "it must be admitted that public opinion in France — even on the Left — was for the present strongly against the application of naval sanctions to Italy." At the Congress of the French Radical Party, held several weeks later, nobody went so far as to advocate military sanctions if necessary: "the question was carefully evaded" (*MG.* 26.x). By threatening war and capitalizing the fact that many people believed him capable of any aberration, Mussolini had succeeded in cowing everybody in France. The campaign waged by his hirelings had created unanimity against military sanctions.

In England, the Labour Party was overwhelmingly in favour of military sanctions. As Churchill writes:

A very strong desire to fight the Italian Dictator, to enforce sanctions of a decisive character, and to use the British fleet, if need be, surged through the sturdy wage-earners. Rough and harsh words were spoken at excited meetings. On one occasion, Mr. Bevin complained that "he was tired of having George Lansbury's conscience carted about from conference to conference." . . . On October 8, Mr. Lansbury resigned his leadership of the Labour Parliamentary Party, and Major Attlee, who had a fine war record, reigned in his stead.

At its national conference, the Labour Party gave 2,168,000 votes in favour of a resolution supporting military sanctions, with 102,000 against (October 20).

The British Conservatives could, therefore, play the French Socialists against the British Labourites, besides insisting on the duty to avoid general war. The moment propitious for a general election was approaching. The parliamentary correspondent of the London *Sunday Times*, who expounded the Tory point of view, warned that the election could not be postponed: "sanctions against Italy might fail" (12.x). M.P. Amery welcomed the election because he was sure that the electorate would give the Conservative majority "a very definite mandate, not for intensifying the international crisis, but for putting the brake on Mr. Eden's activities at Geneva and getting out of the present entanglement as best we can" (*Evening Standard*, 13.x). Augur also explained that the Conservative Party needed to get the election over "before public opinion understood the extent of the failure of the policy pursued at Geneva." The Conservative Party had to try to capture voters who might shift their weight to the Left Parties, and this could be done only by snaring the vast current of opinion that had manifested itself in the peace ballot. . . .

Between Labourites and Conservatives, the British Liberals were wavering. The *Manchester Guardian*, the newspaper with the most consistent record in the campaign for the Covenant and for sanctions, found a certain measure of comfort in the fact that "the pressure of *moral and economic* forces, steady, patient, and persistent," would be tried (26.ix). Thus it, too, gave up military sanctions.

While waiting for the "honourable compromise" announced by Augur to materialize, the Council of the League at Geneva set up another committee, the "Co-ordination Committee," and entrusted it with the task of framing those sanctions which would end the war to everyone's satisfaction.

The new Committee was a diplomatic conference legally distinct from the League itself. It was made up of the delegates of the fifty Governments which had voted for the October 11 declaration: it had no au-

thority to take any decision whatsoever, but was only empowered to list the measures to be submitted to each Government for its approval. The name itself—"Committee of Co-ordination"—showed that it had no authority of its own. It could only co-ordinate proposals freely made by the different Governments through their delegates.

This mass meeting of diplomats naturally chose a sub-committee of eighteen to do the job, and these eighteen split up into three minor committees.

The chairmanship of the several committees was allotted to representatives of small Powers who could only tend, not direct, the machinery. The method adopted throughout the controversy was for the Committee of Eighteen to frame proposals for the decision of the Committee of Co-ordination subject to guidance by the Council. This machinery of joint action started as soon as it was fueled with will power. It ran just as far as the fuel lasted, then stopped; and, thereafter, except for some doleful whistles intended to call attention to its existence, remained stationary.

The work of the Committee was summed up as follows by a member of the French delegation: "Collective enthusiasm, but individual coolness" (*MG.* 16.x). And Low, in one of his famous cartoons, depicted Laval asking Sir Samuel Hoare and Eden: "It is time to padlock the stable door, is it not?" Answer: "But no, the horse is not yet quite flown."

The Committee of Eighteen were concerned (or made a pretence of being concerned) lest Germany, not being bound by the League, should pour unrestricted quantities of sanctioned material into Italy. Unfortunately for the Committee, the Berlin Government informed the Secretariat of the League that Germany would ship into Italy only "normal quantities" of various commodities. It is plain that Mussolini had not yet joined hands with Hitler, and Hitler was forcing his hand. Therefore the Committee had no alibi at its disposal. But piling up legal technicalities it arrogated to itself not only the job of co-ordinating the application of sanctions, but also that of indicating which sanctions were to be applied. In doing this it ignored the League Covenant, which in Article 16, paragraph I, ruled that should any member of the League resort to war in disregard of its Covenant, *all* other members of the League were pledged immediately to sever *all* trade and financial relations and to prohibit *all* intercourse between their nationals and the nationals of the Covenant-breaking State. The words "immediately" and "all" did not allow for loopholes. But the task of experts and committees has always been that of discovering loopholes. Moreover, the Coordination Committee, though sitting in Geneva, did not depend on the League; it could therefore ignore the Covenant.

After making short work of the Covenant, the Committee decided that each Government was bound to apply sanctions only if it deemed them necessary, but it could not take unilateral initiatives which might go beyond those sanctioned by the Committee. The famous "untrammelled national sovereignty" remained untrammelled for whoever did not wish to apply sanctions, but if any Government felt that the sanctions agreed upon at Geneva did not go far enough, it could not go beyond the limits set at Geneva: its national sovereignty was no longer untrammelled. "All the fifty States must keep in step, like dancers on the stage, lest the performance of one might surpass that of the others." As a result, if anyone in England protested that the sanctions were ineffectual, Eden could silence him by pointing out that the Committee had decided thus, and that anyone devoted to the "principle" of "collective" action was bound to obey the "League of Nations."

The Committee never considered the closing of the Suez Canal, not because "so radical a measure would certainly have provoked a war with Italy, and perchance even a world war," but because as late as September 10, that sanction had been explicitly ruled out. Marquis de Vogüé, President of the Commission in charge of the Canal's finances, declared that he felt "the most cordial feeling of friendship" for Italy, and that nothing short of force on the part of Great Britain could have prevented Italy from using the Canal.

Together with the Suez Canal, the oil sanction went overboard. . . .

THE ANGLO-FRENCH "SOLUTION"

As early as October 16, Mussolini had expressed his readiness to negotiate (on his own terms, of course). A peace that had been accepted by Mussolini as well as by Haile Selassie could not be other than "honourable." What objections could be raised against such a peace by those Englishmen who had taken part in the peace ballot, or those delegates who had condemned Mussolini in Geneva on October 11? Could they compel Mussolini and Haile Selassie to remain at war even after they had decided to make peace?

The "League" had not been able to prevent war. Its duty was now to work out a peace settlement. The peace treaty would be signed in the Palace of the League. It would thus be arrived at "within the framework of the League," and "the League" would score the greatest triumph in its history.

Before the end of October, while the election campaign in England was in full swing, Sir Samuel Hoare instructed the British Minister to Addis Ababa, Sir Sidney Barton, to urge upon Haile Selassie "the advisability of his consenting to start peace negotiations for a settlement by compromise"; "Abyssinia's military prospects were even darker than they appeared to be to observers without inside knowledge." Augur was in position to cable to the *New York Times* (30.x) that Sir Maurice Peterson was back from Paris, where, together with French experts, he had found "a formula representing a joint Anglo-French effort to solve the trouble in a way satisfactory to the League of Nations, Italy, and Ethiopia together." Sir Samuel Hoare was making sure that nothing would happen "to wreck irrevocably the prospect for the

Italo-Ethiopian peace settlement." Europe had to be freed from the incubus of "a catastrophic upheaval." "Respect for the Covenant of the League must be upheld, but the Government would not allow the letter to come before the spirit of the document." "A bottomless abyss" yawned before the British and French statesmen "into which they were in danger of slipping." The London *Daily Herald* (30.x) announced that Sir Maurice Peterson and his French opposite number, Count de St. Quentin, had drawn up a plan which needed only British approval before being submitted to the League; this plan met on the whole the demands made by Mussolini two weeks earlier.

Sir Samuel condemned "whispers and innuendos" and left for Geneva. In Geneva he had a meeting with Laval, Aloisi, and the Belgian delegate, Monsieur Van Zeeland (November 1). On the following day the Co-ordination Committee adopted November 18 as the date for putting into effect the sanctions already agreed upon. But when the delegates were about to leave, Monsieur Van Zeeland abruptly proposed that the British and French Governments "should be entrusted with the mission of seeking, under the League's auspices and control and in the spirit of the Covenant, the elements of a solution acceptable to the League of Nations, Italy and Ethiopia." The object of this proposal, which obviously had been concocted at the meeting of the previous day, was to make the League responsible for what had been prepared behind the scenes. However, the Co-ordination Committee had been set up to study the enactment of sanctions, and not to promote conciliation. Van Zeeland's proposal could have been discussed only by the Council or the Assembly of the League. It was therefore only recorded in the minutes, and that was all. Thereafter Sir Samuel Hoare and Laval assumed that the Van Zeeland proposal "represented the unanimous sense of the meeting," whereupon the newspapermen who belonged to the combine announced that Hoare and

Laval had received "a moral mandate" from "the League" to negotiate. . . .

The Hoare-Laval Plan was a great triumph for Mussolini. First of all it upset the time-table of sanctions. Moreover, he was given the right to annex half of Ethiopia. As the Italian Fascist organ in France, *La Nuova Italia*, wrote (12.xii), the offer proved that "the two great Powers knew that Italy was not the aggressor." "We have never heard that conciliatory proposals are made to aggressor nations." If Mussolini had accepted the plan, the English electorate and the House of Commons would have been confronted with a *fait accompli*. Peace would have ensued, and peace — even if it is a bad peace — is always preferable to war, especially if others pay the price. . . .

As was to be expected, in Paris the Press that favoured Laval and Mussolini was glad to note that the British Government had gone much farther along the path of concession "than could possibly have been expected a few days ago"; Mussolini would undoubtedly accept such a generous offer (*LT*. 10.xii). The slogan of the Mussolinian agents was, "Are you willing to die for the Negus?" (*MP*. 10.xii). Three years later Hitler's agents were to ask, "Are you willing to die for Danzig" or "for Czechoslovakia?" Then the moment was to come when they would ask, "Are you willing to die for France?"

The Left-wing Press in France was bewildered and silent. Till then it had sided with the British against Laval. How could it now be more royalist than the King?

In Geneva the plan was received with indignation. The correspondent of the *New York Times*, C. K. Streit, learned from three reliable independent quarters — and he was never contradicted — that the British Government, after getting the promise of assistance from the Governments of the Eastern Mediterranean, had asked them to make known this position to Mussolini. They were on the point of doing so when the news of the Hoare-Laval plan came to "astound them and stop them in their tracks." In addition, they were informed that the British Government had already made known their attitude to Mussolini. "This greatly increased their bitterness, for it seemed to them that Britain had dangerously exposed the weak States to Italy's future wrath and had then deserted them" (22.xii).

In the United States the movement of those who were seeking cooperation with the League of Nations broke down completely.

The Hoare-Laval Peace Plan caused a revulsion of American feeling; for it was interpreted as a sign that the principles of international justice counted far less among the leading members of the League than the safeguarding of their own vital interests and the preservation of the European balance of power. American isolationism exchanged its mood of repudiating the profits to be made out of other people's war for a mood of refusing any co-operation with the League. . . .

In the House of Commons, as soon as the Paris papers reached London in the afternoon of December 9, protests broke out on all sides, even among the ranks of the Conservatives. The *New York Times* correspondent stated that Eden, who "had been fighting (!) for the cause of the League since the Ethiopian crisis had arisen, was furious over what seemed to be a betrayal of everything he had stood for."

Mr. Eden's friends among the Conservatives urged him to resign. At first the proposal seemed to appeal to him as the only way to save his self-respect. But it was announced on his behalf just before the Commons adjourned at 11 o'clock tonight that he would not resign, and would go to Geneva. . . . Prior to this announcement, Mr. Eden had been summoned to Buckingham Palace for a talk with the King.

The fact is that as late as December 5, in the House of Commons, he had protested against rumours that he did not agree with Sir Samuel Hoare and the other members of the Cabinet. There had never been

"the faintest shadow of difference" between him and Sir John Simon or between him and Sir Samuel Hoare. He had always received "the most splendid and loyal help" from his colleagues. "To pretend anything else is singularly insulting to myself, for if in truth I had been in constant disagreement with my colleague, what a poor sort of creature I must be still to be occupying my position on this bench."

Next day the storm broke. In the House of Commons Baldwin began by stating that the Co-ordination Committee "had approved negotiations." The Committee, as we have seen, had no power to take such a step; it had merely listened to Van Zeeland without reaching any decision. Next Baldwin affirmed that "no suggested basis had at present been submitted to the views of either Italy or Abyssinia"; — as if, in the hurry to get Mussolini's consent, no one had thought of telling Baldwin what was being cooked up. Baldwin then announced that he had not yet examined the Press reports, but "he had been told by those who had studied the original proposals and the Press reports that there were considerable differences in the matter of substance." His statements were summed up as follows in the *Manchester Guardian*: "He knew nothing, he had heard nothing, he had read nothing, he said nothing" (12.xii).

When Eden's turn came, he repeated that the Co-ordination Committee had "specifically approved of attempts to find a basis of discussion between the two parties"; as a consequence, "with the knowledge and approval of our fellow-members of the League," negotiations were started; "clearly, that was the course which the League approved, the course which we have followed"; — Monsieur Van Zeeland had become "the League." But Eden had to recant: "We have no mandate from the League, because the Committee had no power to give us one"; but "after an expression of opinion such as was given at the Committee of the League, it was not possible for us to sit still and do nothing." In any event, the plan published by the papers was "only a beginning," a "basis for negotiations." He had not had time to look at the reports "in all the papers" (did he need to read *all* the papers?), but in all those he had seen there were "inaccuracies, important inaccuracies, and many of them were mutually contradictory." His Majesty's Government were not in a position to make the proposals under discussion public owing to the fact that they had not been dispatched to either of the parties to the dispute; he forgot to add the word "officially." All the League Committees — the "Committee of Five, the Committee of Thirteen, and others" — should be informed and have a share in the negotiations before all documents were made public. — He was trying to gain time in the hope that he might be able to announce that the plan had been accepted by the parties to the dispute:

Let us be frank about this: let us face the facts. If Italy and Abyssinia and the League accept to discuss on the basis of this suggestion made in Paris, there is nobody here who is going to say No, even if some of those proposals may not be particularly appealing to us.

Nobody spoke in the Government's defence.

Baldwin had to rise again, and the best argument he found was: "My lips are not yet unsealed." Never in the years that followed did Baldwin explain what lay behind those words, nor has anyone fathomed the mystery. The most plausible explanation is that, having no explanation at hand, he resorted to the trick of sealing his lips in order not to reveal a non-existent reason. From that day onwards, Low's cartoons pictured Baldwin with lips sealed.

His seal, however, did not prevent Baldwin from uttering a half-truth: "So far as *I know* no communications of any kind have gone either to Addis Ababa or to Rome." In truth, Baldwin spoke at 9:47 p.m., and the official telegrams advising acceptance of the proposals were dispatched to Rome and Addis Ababa after the House of Commons had risen. Baldwin went on that as British Prime Minister, he was not necessarily officially informed of what Laval might confidentially have told Mussolini. In Naples they say: "God save us from the lie of an honest man."

THE ETHIOPIAN WAR—AN ITALIAN VIEW

LUIGI VILLARI

> The wide reputation enjoyed by Benito Mussolini in the pre-Ethiopian era as a forceful, astute, but essentially reasonable revisionist is difficult today to comprehend. The name Mussolini has come to conjure up the mountebank, the blustering improvisor, who was overly persuaded by his own salestalk. But apologists for Il Duce aver that his sincere if realistic blueprint to preserve the peace was the victim of narrow imperialist and liberal democratic hostility. Luigi Villari, a well-known Italian historian, was active in various capacities within the Italian Foreign Office for over thirty years until his retirement in 1938. He has become without doubt the most articulate spokesman for the Fascist position on international diplomatic development in the period between the two World Wars.

Barthou's visit to Rome had been announced in October, 1934, but the French Foreign Minister himself was, as we have seen, one of the accidental victims of the Marseilles outrage. Conversations in Rome with a member of the French Government were thus adjourned, and a Cabinet crisis in France caused further delay, Gaston Doumergue having resigned the premiership. His successor, Pierre-Etienne Flandin, chose Pierre Laval for the Quai d'Orsay, and the new Foreign Minister was just as eager as his predecessor for a better understanding with Italy. As soon as the internal situation was cleared up, he departed for Rome and met Mussolini on January 5, 1935. At the Palazzo Venezia banquet on that evening Mussolini in welcoming Laval said that his visit was a clear sign of a Franco-Italian *rapprochement*, which both Laval and his predecessor and he, himself, had long ardently desired, "having in view certain common objectives transcending the sphere of Franco-Italian relations and rising to a higher significance in a European sense

. . . It is not a question, with regard to Central Europe, of renouncing our respective friendships; we are to harmonize in the Danube basin the vital necessities and interests of individual states with those of a general nature, with a general pacification as our aim."

Laval replied in a similar tone, saying: "You are the head of a great country on which you have been able, with your authority, to confer the finest page in the history of modern Italy. Placing your prestige at the service of Europe, you will give an indispensable contribution to the maintenance of peace . . . Before the vestiges of ancient Rome let us swear not to allow humanity to fall once more into the obscurity that so many past centuries have known."

During the visit an agreement between France and Italy was concluded (January 8th) dealing with Italian policy in East Africa and the position of Italian citizens in Tunisia.

Apart from other questions, Laval's visit cleared the air with reference to Franco-

From Luigi Villari, *Italian Foreign Policy Under Mussolini* (New York, 1956), pp. 123–124, 134–136, 138–141, 151–161, 195. Reprinted by permission of the Devin-Adair Co., New York. Copyright 1956.

Italian relations in general. Italy obtained for Libya an extension of territory amounting to 114,000 square km. and another for Eritrea of 1,000 square km., but these were vast almost uninhabited sandy wastes of purely geographical import. Italy also secured an interest of 20 per cent in the Jibuti–Addis Ababa railway. On the other hand, Italy agreed to renounce the Italian citizenship of her settlers in Tunisia within 30 years, to allow the Gallicizing of the Italian schools in 20 years and to abandon all general claims over Tunisia.

In view of these important concessions, Laval had given Mussolini, so far as France was concerned, a free hand in Ethiopia, with which Italy's relations at that time had begun to be difficult. At a later date the British Foreign Minister, Anthony Eden, declared that Laval had assured him that he had spoken of "a free hand" only in the economic sphere. Laval, himself, in a letter sometime later, asserted that he had actually used the expression "a free hand" without any qualifications, so that it might be interpreted either in a political or an economic sense. It is not likely that Mussolini would have surrendered the rights of the Tunisian Italians on so large a scale unless he was convinced that he had secured an adequate *quid pro quo*.

Collaboration between France and Italy seemed at last to be assured — "the greatest service rendered to the cause of peace," as the eminent Swiss publicist Paul Gentizon wrote, "since the first World War." . . .

During the period [that followed], Hitler had undertaken the cancellation of the more burdensome limitations imposed on Germany at Versailles. In March, 1935, he re-established compulsory military service and raised the nation's peacetime effectives to 36 divisions. These moves were not wholly approved by Mussolini. Although he had always been favorable to treaty revision, he did not consider that it should be effected unilaterally, and he still believed that Italy, Great Britain and France should collaborate to keep the peace in Europe.

France was eager that a meeting should be held in Italy between French, British and Italian representatives to deal with the situation generally and especially with the German problem. This scheme was discussed in Paris (March 24th) at a preliminary meeting between Laval, the British Minister for League Affairs, Anthony Eden, and the Italian Undersecretary for Foreign Affairs, Fulvio Suvich. From this conversation it was evident that the British Government was trying to avoid a meeting in Italy, so as not to offend the susceptibilities of the Liberal-Labor Opposition, which hated the Fascist regime. But at the same time the British Government sought to contact the even more totalitarian regimes of Germany and Russia, sending the Foreign Secretary, Sir John Simon, to Berlin and Eden to Moscow.

Having failed to arrive at any definite conclusions in either capital, the British Government agreed to the meeting in Italy, which took place at Stresa from April 11th to 14th and was attended by MacDonald, Simon, Flandin, Laval, Mussolini and various officials. From the first moment, MacDonald showed great consideration for Germany; and if Laval appeared more uncompromising, it was only because he hoped thus to arrive at a lasting arrangement with Hitler. Mussolini predicted that the Führer's next move would be the occupation of Austria, and he reminded his hearers of Italy's vigorous action to safeguard Austrian independence after the murder of Dollfuss, an action not supported by the Western powers.

A "Stresa front" was vaguely talked about and Great Britain and France invited Italy to join in a guarantee to keep Germany in restraint. Yet, at this very same time they were also contemplating sanctions against Italy in regard to the Ethiopian affair.

While agreements were arrived at on various minor matters, nothing was concluded on the main point, a common and definite line of policy toward possible German aggression. The British delegates limited themselves to saying "Naughty, naughty!" to Hitler.

The Ethiopian question, over which British public opinion and, to some extent, the British Government were getting excited, was not discussed at all by the delegates. It was only casually talked about by some of the British and Italian officials.

Two months after Stresa, Great Britain, without consulting France or Italy, concluded an agreement with Germany authorizing the Reich to build a fleet including submarines, in flat violation of the Versailles Treaty. Laval was very indignant with the British, but the Foreign Office replied that Great Britain would lend France support in the North Sea provided that France undertook to support the British position in the Mediterranean — evidently against Italy. Laval brought this out at the Pétain trial, where he also revealed that in 1934 secret military agreements had been concluded between France and Italy in case of German aggression.

It was only when the results of the Peace Ballot (a sort of referendum organized by the British League of Nations Union) were published and seemed to prove the existence of League fanaticism in millions of British subjects (including infants and lunatics), that the Baldwin Cabinet decided that it must adopt a 100 per cent League policy if it was to win the next election. No member of the Government seems to have realized that the ballot was one of the most colossal frauds of modern times. It is at this moment that the real quarrel between Italy and Great Britain began, the British Government being convinced that it must uphold League principles at any cost, even a world war.

In the spring of 1935 it was suggested in certain British quarters that Italy might be given a position in Ethiopia similar to that of Great Britain in Egypt. Mussolini replied that this idea was by no means without merit. Perhaps a solution on that basis might have been reached at that time, but Stanley Baldwin afterwards repudiated it, fearing that it would prove distasteful to the League of Nations Union. France, too, had suggested an Italian mandate over Ethiopia, and Italy would have considered this favorably before developments had reached a point of too serious tension.

The first definite proposal for a solution was presented on behalf of the British Government by the Minister for League of Nations Affairs in the Baldwin Cabinet, Anthony Eden, who visited Rome in June, 1935. But it was very different from the suggestions and assumptions of the Maffey report. Ethiopia was to give the Ogaden province to Italy, and Great Britain was to compensate Ethiopia by giving it Zeila and a corridor to that port, so that the Negus could have access to the sea.

The proposal did not prove satisfactory to Italy, for it would have provided Ethiopia with ample facilities for the traffic in arms from Europe and slaves from Arabia. These were the only real objects of the Ethiopian demand for access to the sea, its legitimate foreign trade being negligible. It would have opened the door for the direct intervention in Ethiopia of other countries — Russia, for instance. On the other hand, the permanent Ethiopian menace to the security of Italy's existing colonies would have remained unaltered. In exchange Italy would only have secured more waste lands to add to her already superabundant "collection of deserts," as Mussolini called it.

In Great Britain, even this plan was very unfavorably received. The idea of giving away even a small fraction of British territory was regarded by the imperialists as intolerable; and that of making even a minimum concession to Fascist Italy seemed monstrous to Liberals, Laborites and League partisans.

In any case Mussolini rejected the plan as wholly inadequate, and this refusal had a profound effect on Eden, puffed up as he was with the fatuous vanity of a second-rate mind. He was unable to get over the idea that a proposal made by *him* could be turned down, and he never forgave Mussolini or Italy for this snub. Always after that time he devoted his every effort to get condign punishment inflicted on the Italian people and its chief statesman. . . .

We do not know exactly when Mussolini first contemplated drastic operations in East Africa and the occupation of Ethiopia, or a protectorate over it. He does not seem to have thought of it before the Wal-Wal incident, even though in a general way he was always obsessed by the compelling problem of finding some outlet for Italy's superabundant population. A more intensive development of Libya might have been a partial solution, and he did, indeed, undertake a large-scale scheme of that kind, which soon began to convert the North African colony into a prosperous domain. But the danger to the small Italian colonies in East Africa from Ethiopian raids and the possibility of settling a large number of Italians in Ethiopia itself, first through some understanding with the Negus, suggested to his mind the idea of a more drastic solution. Had it not been for the Wal-Wal episode, which convinced him that no satisfactory agreement could be reached with Ethiopia as it then was behaving, relations with that country might have remained peaceful, at least for a very long time.

If the Ethiopian Government had allowed Italian economic activities to develop freely, and if it had appointed a certain number of Italian experts in the various technical public services as it had undertaken to do under the terms of the treaty of 1928, Italian penetration might have developed peacefully without a war and with beneficial results to all concerned.

There were no Ethiopians capable of carrying out important technical work, and foreigners had to be employed. Yet even after the 1928 treaty, when large numbers of European advisers were actually appointed, only one of them (an electrical engineer) was an Italian. An Englishman was selected as adviser for internal administration, one Frenchman for public works, another for archeological research, and a third for foreign affairs (supplanted later by a Swede), another Swede for military

affairs, other Frenchmen and Germans for aviation, a Swiss for legal affairs and an American for finance.

But the Wal-Wal episode and other subsequent acts of violence by Ethiopians had brought the relations between the two countries to a state of acute tension, which was rendered more serious by the intervention of the British Government, or at least by its agents, in East Africa who, openly or clandestinely, encouraged resistance to all Italian claims. There can be no doubt that it was these events that gradually brought Mussolini around to the idea of a plan for converting Ethiopia into an Italian colony or protectorate. The direct or indirect responsibility of British action for the events that followed is well established.

It is possible that Mussolini might have secured the results desired by indirect means through a system somewhat like that adopted by Great Britain in Egypt and elsewhere, which, as we have seen, had been suggested. He could have claimed to be acting on behalf of the *real* interests of the natives, camouflaging imperialistic ambitions under the guise of humanitarianism, of the defense of international law and so on. He might also have found plenty of arguments in support of his policy in the League Covenant. Possibly, the methods he followed may have been faulty, too direct, too logical, too outspoken. He never concealed his plans or his policy, and indeed, he did in 1935–1936 only what Great Britain, France, Spain, Portugal, Holland, Belgium, the United States, not to speak of Russia, had done in the past. Moreover, he acted as he did at a time when Italy's need for a population outlet was greater than that of any other country.

Had not Hailé Selassié been encouraged by Great Britain, he might well have come to terms with Italy and secured for himself a position like that of the Khedive of Egypt under Great Britain or of the Bey of Tunis under France. Even now that he has been reinstated on his throne by the Allied armies, he is in the position of a poor relation dependent on the grudging goodwill and the skimpy generosity of his British "protectors." He may, indeed, now regret that he did not come to terms with Mussolini when it was still possible. But, of course, all this lies now in the realm of the might-have-been. . . .

It should be borne in mind that the idea of occupying and colonizing Ethiopia enjoyed very wide popularity in Italy. The compelling need for more land was keenly felt by all classes. It was not mere greed for colonies, but an urgent necessity. Even many of the opponents of the Mussolini regime were less hostile to the Ethiopian enterprise than to any other measure of the Fascist Government. It was well known that the Ethiopian uplands contained far more land than the natives in their primitive conditions could possibly occupy or cultivate. There was, indeed, room for many hundreds of thousands of Italian families in the country without encroaching on the small area farmed by the Ethiopians. . . .

*　*　*

[Once Mussolini had invaded Ethiopia, the League proclaimed Italy the aggressor and applied a variety of economic sanctions.] The day before sanctions came into force the British Government attempted to force non-League countries to issue certificates of origin for all goods exported to Great Britain, so as to be certain that they did not come indirectly from Italy. The demand was, however, rejected by the governments concerned as an intolerable interference in their own affairs; and in the end considerable quantities of Italian goods were actually admitted into Great Britain *via* neutral countries. Cargoes of lemons, for instance, were landed in British ports as coming from Norway or Iceland. On the other hand, on one occasion, 100 Rolls-Royce motors for war aeroplanes were landed at Spezia for the Italian air force. Sometimes, even under sanctions, business is business.

The League Powers other than Great Britain were not at all keen about sanctions

and had only agreed to them under intense British threats. In France, Laval continued to maintain his strong opposition to them, although even he did not dare to irritate the British too much. He tried hard to work out some solution which might appear to have a League character, again suggested an Italian mandate over Ethiopia, and made other conciliatory proposals. But he always found the British uncompromising. At a public dinner some years later (June 28, 1939) he said: "It was in order not to break with Great Britain and the League that sanctions were applied. It was in order not to break with Italy and provoke a war, at that time practically certain, that sanctions were applied with moderation."

French public opinion and most of the press were openly anti-sanctionist, and there were violent public demonstrations against sanctions. The British tried to stop the publication of pro-Italian articles in certain French newspapers, such as *Gringoire,* and the British Embassy protested indignantly against Henri Béraud's fiery attacks on British policy. . . .

We now come to the most extraordinary episode in the whole Ethiopian conflict — the Hoare-Laval plan.

Italian military operations having begun very successfully, the British Government, while trying desperately to enforce a solution by means of ever more severe sanctions, now had an inkling as to the advisability of trying a more conciliatory settlement in agreement with France, which asked for nothing better. A first proposal was suggested at Geneva by a British Foreign Office official to the Italian diplomat, Renato Bova-Scoppa, whereby some territorial concessions would be granted to Italy in exchange for an Ethiopian outlet to the sea. Italy's repeated military victories had convinced Laval that a solution really acceptable to that country must be found, and he invited Hoare to come over to Paris to discuss the matter with him. Hoare accepted the invitation, for he feared that, if the oil embargo against Italy then being discussed in League circles was applied, it might give Italy an excuse for attacking the British fleet in the Mediterranean. He was also anxious about the increase of the German navy that the British Government had authorized and about the possibility of an Italo-German agreement on Austria and other matters.

The Hoare-Laval meeting took place early in December 1935, to discuss the plan in strict secrecy; but there were soon "leaks" by two left-wing French journalists, *Pertinax* and Genevieve Tabouis, and news also reached *The Times* of London. On December 8th the London *Observer* published a scheme whereby Italy was to receive the non-Amharic ("colonial") territories of Ethiopia, which Mussolini had claimed previously, a plan alleged to have the support of the British Colonial Office, always less anti-Italian than the Foreign Office. But in League circles the mere suggestion of a conciliatory solution still aroused outbursts of hysterical indignation.

It was not known at the time that before leaving London Hoare had instructed Rex Leeper, of the Foreign Office Press Section, to prepare public opinion for lifting the sanctions. Leeper replied that this would require a month's work, but Hoare insisted that it must be done before the Geneva Council meeting scheduled for December 12th.

The plan arranged by Hoare and Laval was communicated to Mussolini by the British and French ambassadors in Rome, with the request that he should declare as soon as possible whether he was prepared to negotiate on that basis. The joint note proves that the plan was the proposal not merely of Hoare and Laval personally, but of the British and French governments. The idea was that Eastern Tigrai and other territories be ceded to Italy and that Ethiopia be given an outlet to the sea at Assab in Eritrea. In Northern Ethiopia, Italy then would have an area assigned to it for economic development and colonial settlement, but operating under a League scheme of assistance in which Italy would have a predominant but not exclusive share.

The plan was obviously very complicated and offered infinite possibilities for intrigue and disputes. But it was an improvement over all previous proposals, and it might have served as a basis for discussion, as the Italian Government admitted. In any case, it completely upset the League thesis, for, by admitting Italy's right even to a square mile of Ethiopian territory, it wiped out the charge of Italian aggression and violation of League pledges.

The Addis Ababa Government, to which the plan had been communicated, protested indignantly and demanded that the League Assembly be summoned to discuss it. In the British House of Commons, as soon as some members got wind of the plan, there was an outburst of virtuous indignation. The horrified members of the League of Nations Union rose up in arms, and the Government was much perturbed and frightened. Baldwin did not wish to assume responsibility for rejecting the plan himself, as it was the joint proposal of his whole Cabinet, but he hoped that the League Council would reject it and save him from making himself ridiculous. In the meantime, the British Minister in Addis Ababa, Sir Sydney Barton, encouraged the Negus to reject the plan.

In France, in Government circles and in the country generally, it was hoped that the plan would be accepted. In some other countries, it was regarded with curiosity and with the hope that something might come of it to ease the general tension. In the United States, Secretary Cordell Hull was definitely opposed to it but took no action. In Rome, Mussolini studied the plan very carefully but would make no decision until he had consulted the Grand Council, which was to meet on December 18th, as that body had by law to be consulted on all questions affecting Italian territorial possessions.

The full text, published on December 13th, increased the indignation of British Liberal, Labor and some Conservative circles. A delegation of the League of Nations Union called on Baldwin to protest against the plan. At Geneva the delegates of the smaller powers expressed strong disapproval, but for a different reason. After having been bullied and threatened into sacrificing their interests to suit a purely British policy, they were being let down by the British Government now that it suited its own interests to come to a settlement with Italy.

On the 19th Hoare issued a detailed defense of his action, and Clement Attlee, leader of the Opposition, inveighed against the plan as "a concession to the aggressor." Baldwin, fearing for his majority (which was in no danger whatever) and with a hypocrisy rare even in the politics of Great Britain, now said that he "had never really liked the plan," that on that fatal Sunday it had not been possible for the Foreign Office to communicate with Paris (though there was a quite efficient London-Paris telephone service), and that the outcry against the plan had greatly impressed him. The plan, he said, must be regarded as dead and buried. All this was typical of Baldwin: while posing as the plain, honest, simple English business man who knew hardly anything about politics, he was really a crafty politician who thought of little except manipulating votes and concocting clever intrigues. Hoare then felt obliged to resign from the Foreign Office, and the warmongering Eden was appointed to succeed him. Hoare, who had on the whole been right, was thus forced to go; but Baldwin, who had been wrong, remained, and Eden, who had been still more wrong, came in.

Subsequently, an excuse for the British withdrawal of the plan was based on a speech by Mussolini at Pontinia, and this was the explanation given to me by a member of the British Embassy in Rome. All that Mussolini had said on that occasion was that "we shall not send the flower of our manhood to distant lands if we are not sure that they will be protected by the Tricolor." But Baldwin had announced his intention of withdrawing the plan (which he "had never liked") on the same day and

at the very hour that Mussolini had delivered the Pontinia speech. The real explanation was that Baldwin feared that a considerable section of his own very large majority might go over to the Opposition, and that he might be forced to resign by a hostile vote – in his eyes a far worse calamity than a world war.

Hoare was an honest, well-intentioned and not unintelligent statesman, but somewhat weak and vacillating. The manner in which he announced his resignation was dignified; not so was his defense of his action in the House of Commons or his letter to his constituents. Instead of defending the plan, which was originally that of all the members of the two governments, he seemed eager to prove that it only offered "a very small concession to the aggressor." The late Sir Arnold Wilson, in talking to me about Sir Samuel Hoare, said that he seemed to have been descended from several generations of maiden aunts.

The United States did not take a definite line on the Ethiopian war. But on January 5, 1936, President Roosevelt told Congress that Italy and the other have-not Powers had failed to demonstrate "the patience necessary to attain reasonable and legitimate objects by peaceful negotiations or by an appeal to the finer instincts of world justice," and he somewhat sanctimoniously contrasted these grasping nations with peaceful and moral America. This statement provoked a sharp rejoinder from Mussolini. Although the United States Government did impose certain partial restrictions on trade with Italy, in spite of Ambassador Long's remonstrances and the appeals to the Italo-Americans, the Government resisted the very intense British pressure and refused to take any part in sanctions.

For some time there were no further attempts at a settlement, but there was no tightening up of sanctions such as Eden wished. Laval told Cerruti, the Italian Ambassador in Paris, that decisive Italian military success would be the best help toward a solution. But his own position was now compromised and his resignation imminent. On the eve of retirement, he wrote a letter to Mussolini saying that when (January 1935) he had spoken of a free hand for Italy in East Africa, he meant it only with regard to economic predominance, although this would really have signified in the long run complete Italian domination in every field. The British Secret Service in the meantime had been conducting an active clandestine campaign to get Laval ousted, and it had actually reached the point, as one of the French delegates at Geneva told an Italian colleague, of bribing certain French deputies. The game succeeded, Laval fell, and a *Front populaire* Government, hostile to Italy, came into power.

Italy's victorious progress led, however, as Laval had expected, to a new suggestion for a conciliatory solution. But at a meeting of the Committee of Eighteen on March 2nd Eden, to everyone's surprise, stated that his Government favored an embargo on oil against Italy, provided that all other countries adhered to it. The new French Premier, Flandin, although less friendly to Italy than Laval, succeeded in avoiding an increase in the tension by proposing that the Committee of Thirteen be summoned to seek a new solution. The Thirteen did meet soon after and voted a resolution inviting both belligerents to institute negotions "within the framework of the League and in the spirit of the Covenant." The Negus's acceptance arrived on the 5th and that of Italy on the 7th. This greatly upset the British sanctioners, but other delegates intervened to seek a way out. The Spanish representative, Salvador de Madariaga, tried to act as an intermediary; but after various discussions Eden proposed on April 7th that if hostilities were not suspended at once, the Eighteen should be summoned again to intensify sanctions (another "turn of the screw").

An unexpected move was made by the delegate for Ecuador, Gonzalo Zalumbide, who on that same day announced to the League Council that he had been instructed by his Government to declare that the continuance of sanctions was a menace to world peace, and that other means must be found to secure it. This was the first open challenge, presented by a small South American state, which thus gave a lesson to all other countries and an answer to Eden's bullying—the first sign that the sanctionist front was beginning to crack.

Eden now tried another tack; he accused Italy of having used poison gas in the Ethiopian campaign. Thereupon, it was decided, at Madariaga's suggestion, that a committee of three jurists be appointed to prepare a report on all the violations of the accepted laws of war by both belligerents that would be submitted to the Thirteen, who would study the procedure for a future inquiry. Italy had, in fact, often called the attention of the League to many such violations attributed to the Ethiopians. The League Secretary-General then asked the International Red Cross to supply him with all the information in its possession on that subject, but his request was rejected. Aloisi announced that Italy had used gas only in very few cases, that it had done so chiefly to block certain roads and to prevent their use by the enemy, and that in any case this had only been done several months *after* his Government had submitted a detailed report on the atrocities committed by the Ethiopians (the use of explosive and expanding bullets, etc.)—a report of which not the slightest notice had been taken.

Some officials of the League Secretariat in conversation with the Italians now reverted to the old proposal that Italy be granted in Ethiopia a position similar to that of Great Britain in Egypt—which, incidentally, was quite illegitimate from the point of view of international law. In any case, it was rather late in the day for such a suggestion.

On May 2nd, after an uninterrupted series of Italian victories, a solution was hastened by the sudden flight of the Negus for Palestine. He announced his intention of proceeding thence to London at the invitation of various British associations. Even then, it seems that he actually wished to come to terms with Italy, which would certainly have treated him very generously as a gallant defeated enemy; but the British authorities had spirited him away to keep him in cold storage for future use. There was nothing that was less desirable from a British-Eden point of view than an agreement between Fascist Italy and Hailé Selassié.

The Italian forces, after overcoming the last enemy resistance, reached Addis Ababa on May 5th. The news came as an astounding surprise to many millions of newspaper readers in Great Britain, who had been repeatedly assured for many months by correspondents telegraphing from Ethiopia (or from Khartoum or Cairo or Baghdad or Antofagasta) that the Italians were being held up, that they were dying from disease like flies, that they were being defeated, and that they were in headlong flight. . . .

On May 9th Mussolini announced the annexation of Ethiopia to Italy with King Victor Emmanuel III as Emperor. A new series of debates now started at Geneva, where Eden still rejected any idea of lifting sanctions. But in Great Britain an ever-increasing number of political leaders declared themselves opposed to their maintenance. Baldwin, who always sensed which way the political wind was blowing, admitted the failure of collective security, attributing it to the absence from the League of the United States, Germany, and Japan.

On May 28th even Eden was beginning to change his views. He admitted that Mussolini's conciliatory attitude had influenced the dissension already manifest in Italo-British relations. His own Government, he now said, wished to eliminate the crisis between Italy and the League. But the question now was whether the League could find a way out that would permit a formal if not an honorable liquidation of the past without compromising its existence. Eden ended by confessing — rather late in the day — that the sanctions experiment had failed signally, and that Italian

collaboration was more than ever necessary for the system of collective security in Europe.

In London Vansittart told Grandi that sanctions must be lifted, that the League had proved entirely wrong about Italy, that its face must be saved — and that of Great Britain, too. Sanctions had failed, he finally admitted, because no power except Great Britain was really keen for them.

Count Galeazzo Ciano, Mussolini's son-in-law, who had been Undersecretary for Propaganda since 1934 and Minister in that same Department since 1935, was appointed Minister of Foreign Affairs immediately after the end of the war, on June 9, 1936, a post held until then by Mussolini himself. The choice was variously appraised, for although he was a man of undoubted abilities and a diplomat of experience, Ciano was regarded as too young for so responsible a position, and he had made himself unpopular in many quarters because of certain defects of character.

While the lifting of sanctions was now admitted to be imminent, another difficulty arose over the international recognition of the Italian Empire in Ethiopia. On June 16th Drummond assured Ciano that while the sanctions question was practically settled, recognition could not yet be admitted, and the same opposition arose on the part of some other countries.

The League Council met on June 28th and the Assembly on the 30th. The gathering was now attended by the Negus, where his presence gave rise to much excitement. After some wrangling and bitter disputes, on July 15th a resolution was voted for lifting sanctions, but the Ethiopian proposal that no annexation obtained by force should be recognized was not even put to the vote. The Ethiopian request for a loan of £10,000,000 was rejected by 23 votes and 23 abstentions, with only one vote in favor of it — that of the Ethiopian delegate.

The application to Ethiopia of the same trickery as had been applied to Italy in October, 1935, provided the measure of the meanness and immorality of League methods. The President (the Belgian Paul van Zeeland) interpreted the Assembly's silence as consent to his thesis that the first Ethiopian resolution should not be put to the vote, just as President Beneš had interpreted in a sense hostile to Italy the silence of the Assembly the previous year.

Thus ended one of the most deplorable episodes in politico-diplomatic history: the unsuccessful attempt to starve a civilized nation of 40,000,000 people into surrender. . . .

Some English critics are inclined to throw all the blame for English disasters since 1939 on the shoulders of Winston Churchill. The English monthly magazine, *The European,* observed in an editorial in the issue of May, 1955, that Churchill "found a great Empire and left a small dependency." This is true, but Eden was more responsible than Churchill. But for Eden's blocking of peace moves before 1939, it is likely that there would have been no war in 1939 and Churchill could never have become Prime Minister to bring about the liquidation of the British Empire in large part. In short, Edenism from 1934 to 1938 was responsible for Churchill and the disastrous impact of the latter's policies on Britain, Europe and the world.

FRANCE AND ITALY

ARNOLD WOLFERS

Among the sobering consequences of the peace conference at Versailles not the least was the deteriorating power position of France and her growing political isolation. The series of alliances with the secondary powers of Eastern Europe did not take the place of the former warm relationship with Great Britain and Russia. Relations with Italy, deeply dissatisfied with the Treaty and pursuing a Balkan and Mediterranean policy contrary to the interests of France, were strained. The rise of Nazi Germany, however, made imperative a reappraisal of French policy. Arnold Wolfers, Sterling Professor of International Relations at Yale University, was, before coming to the United States in 1933, director of the *Hochschule fuer Politik* in Berlin. In the following excerpt he makes an objective appraisal of the French position.

THE relations of France with Italy after 1919 were not dissimilar to those with the Soviet Union. This other Great Power on the Continent, another wartime ally of France, was also allowed to remain outside of the French security system until the days of German rearmament. Here again appears a contradiction between the French obsession with guarantees of security and her apparent indifference or ineptitude in the matter of securing closer bonds with Italy. The latter was a co-member of the League and, therefore, committed under Article 16 to participate in League sanctions; but her influence at Geneva and her interest in the League were not great at any time. She was a guarantor of the Franco-German boundary through the Treaty of Locarno; but nothing speaks more clearly of the difference with which she and Great Britain were regarded in Paris than the almost complete lack of any mention of Italy in the many debates on Locarno which took place in the French Chamber. Relations between France and Italy, which had been strained ever since

Italy had left the Versailles Conference dissatisfied and resentful, remained tense all through the pre-Hitlerian era.

There were many reasons, some similar to those existing in the Russian case, why France should have been reserved and cautious in her dealings with Italy and should have held back from any serious effort to make her an ally. For once, however, Great Britain was not the stumbling-block. Friendship between the two countries would have been to her interest, if only because it would have removed one of the most serious obstacles to an agreement on disarmament among all of the naval powers. An alliance might have been a different matter, to be regarded with some suspicion by the British, but the likelihood of that was very remote.

As in the Soviet case, differences of ideology and régime had some influence in keeping the two countries apart, only here the roles of the Left and the Right were reversed. The Rightists frequently accused their opponents on the Left of allowing anti-Fascist feelings to poison the atmosphere between the two countries and to stand in the way of friendly settlements.

Another factor which we have encountered in the Russian case played an even more significant part here: the opposition of the Little Entente to any close ties between France and Italy. This was not simply a question of rivalry between two groups of potential allies of France. Italy's ambitions ran directly counter to the vital interests of the Little Entente states. What Yugoslavia sought from France was protection against Italy, not against Germany. Italian support of Hungarian revisionism, as well as of the Bulgarians and Macedonians, her desire to make the Adriatic an Italian sea, the sympathies which she showed at times for a Hapsburg restoration, and her penetration into Albania were all threats to one or another of the Little Entente powers.

But the decisive obstacle to co-operation between France and Italy lay in the fact that Italy, unlike Poland or the Little Entente, was a dissatisfied country and could not be attracted to France by mere guarantees of the established order. She was out for change, not for the enforcement of the *status quo,* and many of the changes which she desired could be effected only by far-reaching French concessions. This placed France in a most serious quandary. It may have taken her a long time to realize the seriousness of the situation, since the French tended to under-estimate the potential military and political value of Italy. But she could not have ignored the menace that might some day arise if a power of the size and energy of Italy were allowed to remain unfriendly and hostile. There could be no question of pushing Italy out of Europe as had been attempted with the Soviet Union. By her geographical position and her interests she belonged in the very heart of European affairs. The danger of an alignment with Germany may have seemed less than in the case of the Soviet Union, since Austria seemed to be an ideal apple of discord. This possibility existed, nevertheless, and it compelled France to

choose between making sacrifices to Italy or to risk losing her to the German camp.

A country as eager as France for new guarantees of security would certainly have lined up with Italy if only the price had not appeared too great. But more was involved for France than this or that concession, this or that naval agreement, this or that cession of colonial rights or territory. The whole conception of the preservation of the *status quo* could not be harmonized with Italian or Fascist "dynamism" driving for greater power, broader political influence, and larger colonial possessions. Italy's policy may be called imperialist or laid to the need of a newcomer seeking to make up for the advantages already possessed by longer-established empires; she certainly never made any secret of the fundamental objective of her foreign policy. It was the same substantially before, during, and after the World War. This did not mean that Italy was necessarily bent on gaining advantages only at the expense of France; but the increase of power which Italy desired was bound to have unfavorable consequences for France and her allies however it was achieved. It would affect France's influence on the Danube and in the Balkans, her naval superiority over Italy, her traditional role in the Near East, and, finally, the security, if not the size and extent, of her African possessions. It was certain to weaken some of the allies of France. Finally, it involved the risk that precedents would be established which would constitute a threat to the whole program of enforcement of the existing post-war order and territorial *status quo.* Because Italy's aims were "revisionist" they were hostile to the French system of security.

If any French statesmen doubted the seriousness of Mussolini's revisionist policy on the ground that Italy had also profited by the post-war peace treaties and obviously would not allow any changes prejudicial to herself, they were woefully mistaken as to the workings of a revisionist policy. No revisionist country favors the change of all existing boundaries or settlements. It merely insists that some particular changes which it desires and considers justified shall be given precedence over any comprehensive guarantee of the established order. Once these particular changes have taken place, the former revisionist country may well join the *status quo* group and, having become saturated, desire to see the new order enforced. Mussolini, indeed, if we may believe his own statements, was considering this possibility after the conquest of Ethiopia.

Since France was never willing to sacrifice her *status quo* principles or to make any sweeping concessions to Italy for the sake of her friendship and support, the cordiality of the relations between the two countries came to depend on whether Italy would consider waiving or postponing her claims in order to assure herself of French backing. Such support would be important to Italy only if she anticipated the need of assistance against Germany, a need likely to arise only in connection with the problem of Austro-German *Anschluss*.

French policy toward Italy began to change at the same time as that toward the Soviet Union. The coincidence was no accident. In face of the rise of Germany's power the French Government looked for new allies. After preliminary attempts to improve relations with Italy and the Soviet Union had been made in 1933, Barthou, in 1934, set out to forge a new and more powerful ring of continental alliances around Germany with which to supplement the now insufficient "small ring" in Central Europe and to balance the effects of Germany's impending rearmament. Why she found the Soviets in a responsive mood, we have explained. Italy had even more urgent and pressing reasons to fall in with the French plans. The union of Austria and Germany, which Italy had so consistently and vigorously opposed as a threat to her vital interests, seemed to be the first item on Hitler's revisionist program. By July, 1934, with the murder of Dollfuss, a crisis was reached and Italy, it

is said, set out to prevent the *Anschluss* by the threat of armed intervention. Here was an opportunity, if ever there was one, for France to draw Italy into her camp.

Laval and Mussolini signed a series of agreements on January 7, 1935 — the so-called Rome agreements. The French rejoiced in the belief that the alignment of the two countries had been accomplished. In fact, according to Flandin, the French and Italians, a few months later at the Stresa Conference, exchanged definite promises of military assistance, with an Italian promise to defend the demilitarized zone in the Rhineland and a French promise to defend Austria's independence. The short-lived "Stresa front" represented the height of Italian co-operation with the Western democracies and was supposed to inaugurate complete understanding among the three powers both in regard to general policy and future dealings with National Socialist Germany. French Rightist statesmen, who for years had been extremely critical of French foreign policy, hailed the Stresa front as the "safety of Europe" and as "the only true clarity" since Versailles. This enthusiasm and confidence in the newly acquired security shows the significance attached to Italian support, particularly at a time when the French had every reason to be pessimistic, the Stresa Conference having been called for the purpose of dealing with Hitler's proclamation of unrestricted rearmament.

If the published versions of the Rome agreements contained the whole text, France would appear to have been able to satisfy Italy with a minimum of concessions, no more indeed than a modest fulfillment of her part of the promises made to Italy in 1915 and 1917. The Rome agreements therefore represented no break with France's traditional policies, since the transfer of a stretch of desert land could hardly be interpreted as a precedent for any extensive territorial revision. But Italy's claims for empire and for a position of greater power were left unsatisfied. For this reason it has been contended that

Laval must have promised Mussolini more than the published agreements contained, namely, a free hand in Ethiopia. Whether or not this was the case may never be known. If he did, subsequent events proved that France could not break with the past and permit a country to wage a "war of aggression" against another member of the League. If he did not, he was in error in believing that Mussolini could be induced to sacrifice his "dynamic" policy for certain minor concessions and for French support in maintaining the independence of Austria.

While it is of comparatively little importance from the point of view of this discussion whether Laval was guilty of either of these errors of judgment, it is worth mentioning the fact that there are several arguments in support of the assertion that Laval did not give Mussolini a free hand for war on Ethiopia. Laval himself mentioned two. In the first place, France was far too much interested in saving the League from the cataclysm which would follow if Italy were allowed to proceed with a war of conquest. Besides, she was even more interested in preventing Italy from dispatching large armies to Africa when the two countries were just deciding to act jointly in barring German moves in the West and South of Europe. "I would have been imprudent or to blame," Laval said, "if I had facilitated or perhaps provoked who knows what sort of military enterprise in Ethiopia, precisely because this would have deprived us of the presence and the aid of Italy in Europe." There is another argument which Laval did not mention. From the habitual attitude which the French took toward Italy it seems very likely that they underestimated the degree to which Mussolini was committed to a policy of aggrandizement and expansion. It was perhaps too much to expect anyone to foresee that Italy would forfeit her vital defensive or "static" interests on the Brenner for the sake of African conquest. Mussolini did not make it plain until after Stresa that Italy had no intention of keeping her face turned to the

Brenner. Laval therefore acted in harmony with current French conceptions if, as he claimed, "by a formula of economic hands-off" he offered to Italy only "the right to request concessions in Ethiopia while respecting our own acquired rights."

If France was not willing to do more to satisfy Italy, Germany's promises would seem to have gone farther. It seems paradoxical that a "have" country with rich possessions should have been more limited in the concessions it could offer, and therefore find itself in a weaker bargaining position than a "have-not" country. But while France, due to the principles on which her policy rested, could not go beyond the promise of military assistance for the defense of the *status quo* on the Brenner and of certain small concessions, and was not able to fulfill any of Italy's expansionist wishes, Germany needed to have no hesitation in promising Italy compensation for the loss of Austrian independence at the expense of other countries. Italy seems to have believed that German political and military assistance would serve not merely defensive purposes but effectively aid her dreams of empire and expansion. Mussolini in any case chose to risk Italy's position on the Brenner rather than abandon his colonial plans. Possibly he believed that Laval had given his consent, and may have acted under the false impression that Italy would be strong enough to defend Austria even though she engaged herself in Ethiopia and antagonized France. Or he may have decided, on the contrary, that Germany would have her way in Austria anyway, regardless of the steps Paris and Rome might take and may therefore have seen no reason to sacrifice his other plans for a hopeless watch on the Brenner.

At the close of the Ethiopian campaign, it looked for a moment as if Mussolini was ready to listen to French proposals for a resumption of the Stresa policy. Since he had realized his desires for imperial conquest, it would no longer have been inconsistent if for a period of time he had consented to regard Italy as a "saturated" country, and concentrated on blocking the *Anschluss* which he continued to dread. If there was such a moment, France let it slip. The *Front populaire* government then in power did not seek any *rapprochement* with Italy, and could not, Delbos argued, independently recognize the conquest of Ethiopia, "without being remiss to its obligations toward the League of Nations." The clamors of the Rightists that France return to Stresa remained unheard. . . .

Once the opportunity for *rapprochement* had gone by, if indeed it ever existed, the factors drawing Italy away from France (fear of Germany, the growing conviction that Germany could not be restrained in Austria anyway, the "ideological" conflict with France in Spain, the rising tide of Italy's colonial appetite, now turning against French rights and possessions) became stronger and induced Mussolini to side with Germany.

FRANCE BETWEEN TWO WARS

D. W. BROGAN

The Ethiopian Crisis occurred at a time when France, deeply uneasy about developments across the Rhine, was attempting to reconstruct a *cordon sanitaire* against Germany by reapproaching both Russia and Italy. The inner-political problems between Left and Right which were accentuated by this two-pronged advance were cleverly manipulated by Pierre Laval, the man primarily responsible for French policy in 1935. There was a general aura of shiftiness about Laval, and his reputation, abetted by his collaboration with the Germans during the Second World War, is blacker even than that of Mussolini. France was, however, faced with an extraordinary situation in which Laval's peasant cunning could perhaps be accounted the better part of valor. D. W. Brogan, Cambridge don and author of numerous fine studies of France and of the United States, views the French scene dispassionately but with an insider's practiced eye.

Long before 1935, when the Saar plebiscite fell due, few people in France still retained any illusions about the outcome. But for the Hundred Days, the provisions of the first Treaty of Paris in 1814 might have stood and the Saar have been made French in spirit. Over a century of German rule had made the territory as German as Franconia or Brandenburg, and before the rise of Hitler the outcome of the plebiscite was never thought to be in doubt. The Saarlanders would, of course, be making economic sacrifices by leaving the French customs union which permitted the entry of their products, from coal to the excellent Walsheim beer, without any tariff duties. But what were such losses compared with the gain of return to the Fatherland?

The Nazi Revolution seemed to alter things. For one thing, it was notorious that Germany was breaking the disarmament clauses of the Treaty of Versailles. Should she be allowed to benefit by the territorial clauses? The Prussian precedent of Bismarck's refusal to carry out the Schleswig plebiscite might be turned against his heirs. Nobody in France seriously proposed to take so bold a course, but there was surely a possibility that a region so full of Socialists, Catholics and Communists would refuse to vote to put itself under its class and creed enemies? If the plebiscite was safeguarded, it was conceivable that the Saarlanders would vote for the *status quo,* on the understanding that, when Hitler fell, they would be allowed to join a liberated Germany. The security of the plebiscite was, in fact, safeguarded by an international force mainly British, which was impartial, with — French observers thought — a kindly tolerance of the Nazi leaders which might mislead timid Saarlanders. The efforts of the Socialists, the Communists and a few Catholics to secure votes for the *status quo* were not looked on very sympathetically by many Frenchmen; they were not taken much more seriously than

From D. W. Brogan, *The Development of Modern France 1870–1939* (London, 1940), pp. 690–697. Reprinted by permission of Hamish Hamilton Ltd.

were the efforts of a handful of Frenchmen to secure votes for France. If it was true, as the hopeful believed, that Hitler was sincere in his promises of peace and amity after the Saar question was settled, it was to the advantage of France that it should be settled and settled quickly.

The result was decisive enough. Less than 10 per cent voted for the *status quo*, less than 1 per cent for annexation to France. In a predominantly proletarian region, an overwhelming majority had voted for the nation, not for the class. When all allowances had been made for the influence of the Bishop of Trier on the Catholics and for intimidation by the Nazis, the result was, or should have been, of the greatest significance for the leaders of Left parties in France who were still doped with illusions about the artificiality and transitoriness of national divisions. Whatever might be the case in France, it was not true in other countries that more than a handful of the workers were free of the national superstition and conscious only, or mainly, of their common interests as proletarians. And if this was true, the degree to which France had many truly class-conscious proletarians was of the utmost importance.

The question involved was of some urgency for, in France, the effect of the abnormally low birth rate of the war years was now being felt. In face of a rearming Germany what was to be done? Raising the period of army service from one to two years was the Government's solution, a solution opposed with the greatest bitterness by M. Blum and the Socialists. The alleged need for a stronger army, he argued, was the invention of the generals who wanted an aggressive army. The true policy was to agree with the other powers on disarmament and to force the programme of disarmament on Germany. It was an argument directly in line with the Jaurès tradition and it was likely to be electorally profitable (which was not quite out of line with the Jaurès tradition either). For a brief moment the Socialist protest was supported by the Communists. But the Communists had a master who was alive, not in the Panthéon; and on orders from Moscow they withdrew their opposition to a measure which strengthened the military power of a State which, however bourgeois, was about to become an ally of Russia.

Before the Communists had been given their orders, Herr Hitler had taken the occasion to announce openly that he was disregarding the arms limitations of Versailles. That Germany was rearming was no secret. An agreement for mutual air assistance between France and Britain, though not directed against Germany, was not unconnected with the success with which the Nazi Government was restoring the military might of the Reich. The official revelation that Germany had, in fact, created an illegal air force was no news in March 1935, and the further announcement that she was establishing an army whose peace strength was about twice that of the French home strength was alarming, but not unexpected. These unilateral denunciations of treaty obligations were, as the British Government solemnly pointed out, likely to destroy the chances of a "comprehensive agreement." But the German Government was wisely not taking British verbal denunciations at more than their paper value.

The rapid rise of an armed Germany was of interest to more countries than France and Britain. In July 1934, after the blood purge of his party, Herr Hitler's Austrian agents attempted a *coup d'état* which, although successful in removing the obstacle of Chancellor Dollfuss, was otherwise a failure and a failure largely because of the firm resolution of the Duce to oppose, by arms if necessary, so great a menace to Italian security as the establishment of a militant Germany on Italy's northern frontier. The threat to Austria (despite lavish promises and professions of good intentions from Herr Hitler) was driving Italy over to the side of the *status quo* powers. The new director of French foreign policy, M. Pierre Laval, was resolved to keep her there. With Italian support, France could hope to impress on Germany the fact that a new general war and a new defeat would follow a German attempt to undo the territorial settlement of Versailles. If the rulers of Germany were convinced that this was so, there would be no war.

The first steps to winning over Italy had been taken in January when M. Laval had visited Rome. There he believed that he had bought Italian support, or friendly neutrality, by some territorial cessions of not very valuable desert soil, by the transfer of some shares in the Addis-Ababa railway, and by extending until 1965 the right of the Italians of Tunis to have their children regarded as Italian, not as French subjects. It was a good bargain for France, if Italy had indeed been won. But the price was in fact a good deal higher: and the form the price would take was already evident.

In 1934 there had been a frontier fight between Italian and Abyssinian troops at a spot in the debatable land which was probably inside the Abyssinian frontier. The rights and wrongs of the case had been disputed, and Abyssinia which, under Italian patronage, had been admitted to the League of Nations, appealed to Geneva. Various forms of procedure were tried, but the Abyssinians paid less attention to Italian words than to Italian deeds; they noted the increase in Italian military strength on their borders and assumed, rightly, that Italy meant war.

War between two League members was an outrage on all the painfully accumulated post-war hopeful optimism. The French official reaction was to regret that a semi-barbarous state was a member of the League, but even if she were, China had been a member too, and much good had that done her when her fellow-member, Japan, attacked her. The League was not really fit to keep peace all over the world, but it could keep peace where it was most menaced — in Europe. Even if it came to war in Abyssinia, what was at issue? The Abyssinian Empire's independence was almost as much a fiction as the independence of Morocco or Egypt. Alternatively it was by no means certain that its independence *was* menaced, for the Italians had once before found that it was easier to plan the conquest of Abyssinia than to achieve it. The Left, which of all sections in France had the greatest dislike of Mussolini, had also the greatest contempt for the military prowess of the Duce's armies, and it was content to leave the punishment of his temerity to the people immediately concerned — the Abyssinians. M. Laval, at any rate, was very reluctant to lose the fruits of his diplomacy, the separation of Italy and Germany, for such trivial reasons. He asked no awkward questions and it was unnecessary to tell him any lies; to deny, for instance, that war was decided on.

When the British and French Ministers met Signor Mussolini at Stresa, this tactful silence was not broken. The conference was agreed on the necessity of maintaining the integrity of Austria (which meant, if it meant anything, military action by Italy and France) and collective security was to be studied in order to "maintain peace in Europe." There was no mention of peace in Africa; the alarm of the French at the reported views of the British Chancellor of the Exchequer was quieted. All was very satisfactory on paper; preparations were made for a mutual withdrawal of troops from the Franco-Italian border, and M. Laval could regard himself as another Camille Barrère. Italy had been won over. Nor was that all, for on May 2nd the Franco-Soviet pact was signed, and its form having been adjusted to the League system, London had approved. Germany, the treaty-breaker, the menace to the peace of Europe, was indeed encircled. She would not now be subjected to the temptation to use her new armaments to which the chance of a limited war would have exposed her. As Germany was not to be coaxed and cajoled into good behaviour, she must be politely but firmly intimidated.

The apparently sudden interest of the British Government in the Abyssinian question was a shock to M. Laval. He believed that to risk the loss of so important a stabilizing force in Europe as Italy, merely because of formal obligations to Abyssinia, was absurd. Britain had been right when she opposed the entry of Abyssinia into the League, and right when, in 1925, she negotiated with Italy over spheres of influence in Abyssinia in a fashion that showed little respect for the formal sovereignty of the Negus. The sudden British regard for legality, for the sacredness of frontiers, for the sanctity of treaties (which France would have welcomed a few years before) was now suspect. Had it not been imposed on the British Government by the informal plebiscite of the "peace ballot," by those sentimental "clergymen" who, in the eyes of so many Frenchmen, were a danger to the peace of Europe, with their muddled and almost always ill-timed moralization of fundamentally non-ethical problems? M. Laval, too, was peculiarly ill-fitted to understand the British feeling for the small nation attacked by the great, since he, unlike his predecessor M. Barthou, had no great opinion of the smaller allies of France. Europe was ruled by the great powers; that was a fact to be acted on and not a problem in moral philosophy to be debated over.

These were the considerations that, it is assumed, were the basis of the policy of M. Laval. That these considerations were not only those of M. Laval was obviously true. To many, if not to all Frenchmen of the Right, the sacrifice of the new-won friendship of Italy on what they genuinely thought a frivolous or hypocritical pretext, was absurd. To the numerous Fascist sympathizers it was a crime. And to the Frenchmen with a predisposition to admire Italian policy and to covet Italian support, were suddenly added many Frenchmen whose suspicion of the candour of British policy had been aroused by a series of minor pinpricks. Again and again, since Hitler had come into power, the policy of the British Government had seemed to be one of verbal reproof followed by condonation. The Berlin visit of Sir John Simon after the

announcement of German rearmament was not forgotten and it suddenly acquired a sinister appearance when it was announced that, without consulting the other signatories of the Stresa agreements, Britain had concluded a naval treaty with Germany, waiving the restrictions of Versailles and limiting, instead, German surface tonnage to 35 per cent of the British. France felt more than wounded; she felt betrayed. After all the ridicule of French preoccupation with security, Britain had gone behind the back of her former ally and made what was, from her point of view, an excellent bargain, giving her a far greater margin of security than she had had in 1914. France remembered, too, that a deal with Britain as a preliminary to the annihilation of France was a part of the plan of campaign laid down in *Mein Kampf*. The last touch was added by the signing of the treaty on June 18th, the anniversary of Waterloo. Was this a new "Belle Alliance" at the expense of France?

All through the summer of 1935, France, profoundly alarmed and irritated, hoped that she would not have to choose between Britain and Italy, that some face-saving device would be found, but the speech on September 11th of the new British Foreign Secretary, Sir Samuel Hoare, made it plain that France would have to choose, that is, if Britain were *really* going to throw all her strength in support of the League. The British Minister's speech was, indeed, so definite, so positive a commitment of Britain to the principle of collective security, that acute observers in France could hardly believe their ears. A Britain so devoted to the obligations of "full acceptance of League membership" was worth the price of the alienation of Italy. A few years before a French writer on disarmament had pointed out to his countrymen the great merits, from a French point of view, of the obligations of the League system. "The provisions of the Covenant ought to be sacred to us Frenchmen: first of all we reject the theory of 'scraps of paper' — and that means the Treaty of Versailles — then the Covenant makes a comprehensive effort to put an end to the present chaos of international relations by a methodical organization which is both political and juridical. We are attached to peace and the author of the *Discourse on Method* is one of us." But there was little Cartesian rationalism displayed in the last months of 1935.

The cleavage over the Abyssinian question ran through all sections of the country. Despite the outward enthusiasm of the Left for the League and for sanctions, there were many enemies of the internal policy of the Laval Government who privately wished him well in his attempt to avoid estranging either Britain or Italy. The despatch of the British Home Fleet into the Mediterranean encouraged those Frenchmen who were willing to incur risks if Britain were really serious. They told their countrymen that, when she really made up her mind, Britain was unshakable and unbeatable: had she not "had the hide of Napoleon"? On the other hand, if Britain meant business, and that meant war, the timid, the pacific, the prudent and the pro-Italian parties all found themselves united in a common hatred and fear of drastic action. Among the students, the appearance of Professor Jèze of the University of Paris, who had been the counsel for the Emperor of Abyssinia at Geneva, was the occasion of a series of riots which prevented one of the most eminent of French law teachers from lecturing. Among the French Catholics a violent dispute ranged: on one side the supporters of the Duce and on the other the critics of Italian political morality led by M. Paul Claudel, M. François Mauriac and M. Jacques Maritain, a division that was to reappear a few months later in a more profound form over Spain.

The fear of war was the chief argument, the chief emotion to be utilized by Signor Mussolini and his French partisans and employees to weaken the party in favour of the full League policy. The Italian régime was dictatorial; it could not afford to retreat, and its chief had better go down fighting in face of the great powers than be quietly squeezed out of existence by sanctions. Slow sanctions he could ignore for the time being, counting on speedy victory to deliver him from the mild boycott organized from Geneva. Real sanctions, the imposition of impotence on his mechanized troops by holding up the oil supply, that, he gave to understand, meant war. Was France willing to fight a war of which the immediate burden would fall on her (she had a frontier bordering Italy as well as one bordering Germany) for such sentimental reasons as the British Government gave to cover their realist political jealousy of the appearance of a great power on the borders of Egypt?

The newspaper that defended the Italian case and spread the Italian threats went to extremes of abuse that startled even old readers. *Gringoire,* the weekly organ run by M. de Carbuccia (a Corsican clansman-associate of M. Chiappe) was perhaps the most virulent of all the pro-Italian and anti-English journals, but it was a hot race and M. Beraud, the chief mud-slinger of *Gringoire,* only won by a short head.

Mixed up with the question of foreign policy was a question of internal policy. The semi-Fascist parties in France were on the down-grade politically; the approaching elections would inevitably mean a triump for the left, unless the Right could pin on its opponents the deadly charge of war-mongering. And the philosophical Fascists could not afford to see the régime in Italy collapse; its strength, efficiency, and vigour had been the pride of the *Action Française* for over a decade. In Italy, the revolution which M. Maurras had preached was practised.

The great victory of the Baldwin Government in a general election in which the matter of dispute was which side would support the League and the Negus more vigorously, further forced M. Laval's hand, for his opponents, attacking him for many other reasons, could also attack him for his failure to collaborate more warmly with a Government so representative of British sentiment. Indeed, however reluctantly,

M. Laval was bound to follow a strong British lead, unless he could induce Britain to adopt his policy of a compromise that would give the Duce enough to justify a slight retreat on his part. M. Laval thought that such an arrangement was necessary unless Britain was ready to fight, and he asserted that Sir Samuel Hoare from the first had assured him that Britain would not push economic sanctions anywhere near the edge of war.

M. Laval had his way. The world learned through the indiscretion or indiscipline of *Pertinax,* who had consistently opposed the Laval policy of trying to run with the hare and hunt with the hounds, that the brave words of September were being swallowed, that by war and the threat of war, the Duce was getting a great deal of the territory of his fellow-member of the League and of the *Annunziata.* If the Duce had at once accepted the Hoare-Laval plan, the faces of the League and of France and Britain might have been saved. But he waited and British public opinion, less plastic than was necessary, killed the scheme.

All now depended on the prophetic talents of the military experts in France and Britain who calculated on a long and exhausting war in whose course the mild sanctions adopted would, perhaps, be decisive. As the experts were wrong, the defeat of the League and of the two chief powers in it, was made manifest to all the world in the first months of 1936. M. Laval's policy had failed. Italy had been neither conciliated nor intimidated. Britain had not been won over to collective security (the willingness of the Baldwin Government to accept the Hoare-Laval pact, like the failure to impose effective sanctions, showed that); and the British people, whose heart and pride had more been deeply involved than their Government's, were angered at what they thought was a betrayal by France. Even if M. Laval had not failed, elections were near at hand and it was time that the Radicals were back in power, so the Radical Ministers resigned from the Cabinet, which meant that it fell and M. Pierre Laval gave way to a Government headed by M. Albert Sarraut, whose business was to do nothing until the elections in May.

THE LEAGUE RETREATS

SIGMUND NEUMANN

Sigmund Neumann resigned from the *Hochschule fuer Politik* in 1933 on the coming to power of the National Socialists and has since lived an active life as teacher and author at Wesleyan University and as a much-travelled visiting professor in the United States and Europe. Like Toynbee he saw the events surrounding the Ethiopian Crisis as symptomatic of the world's moral malady. Writing in 1946 in the wake of the catastrophic war, he sought to find a meaning to history by analyzing the course of events since 1914. The following selection is taken from his book, *The Future in Perspective*.

WITH the Italo-Ethiopian War, dictatorial aggression moved closer to Europe, testing her powers and finding them devoid of decision and direction. Only if seen as a part of this increasingly tense and desperate drama does the struggle between the Lion of Judah and Il Duce take on its full meaning.

It was more than a case study of a small nation lost against a big one. It became a test of political astuteness and moral fiber of the great powers themselves — and they were found weak. Moreover, it was the League of Nations' second defeat which was the more decisive as Geneva had this time mobilized its machinery against the aggressor and had failed.

To Mussolini, Ethiopia marked the noisy attempt at a renewal of the glory of the Roman Empire. He had been shrewdly biding his time. For ten years he had built up the Fascist chimera. In fact, he was soon so fully established that the forgetful world overlooked castor-oil methods, Matteoti, murder, and Lipari Prison Islands. They still remained of the very essence of fascism. It was not altered by Mussolini's "changing of the guards," putting for a while Farinacci and the other wild boys of

the early hour on the reserve list. Il Duce had given similar advice to Hitler in their first meeting at Venice, 1934, when the Führer was only a junior partner in fascism and, therefore, still listening. The great powers were deceived by these maneuvers because they wanted to be.

By 1933 the respectable democratic press of the Western nations had made Il Duce a respectable statesman. By 1934 he was almost the arbiter of Europe, suggesting the substitution for the League of Nations of a four-power conference, a new concert of nations. The powers had been getting tired of the bothersome League and were quite agreeable to a new Metternich.

Mussolini felt sure that he could capitalize on the extreme unrest of the great powers, in view of the rising Third Reich. In January 1935 he signed with Great Britain and France the Stresa Agreement, which was meant to check Nazi aggression. This did not hinder him in employing this very menace of Hitler as a club for his own plans of aggrandizement. The utter confusion of the Western powers as to what to do when confronted with two centers of disturbance led to Mussolini's initial successes. At the time it looked like adroit

Machiavellian strategy. In historical perspective, it became Mussolini's greatest blunder. It was the beginning of the Rome-Berlin Axis, but by estranging himself from Italy's old allies and by entering the Nazi orbit Mussolini became the prisoner of Hitler. Whoever ate at the New Order's table had to die.

Mussolini meant to be still more clever by preparing his "break-through" with the Franco-Italian Treaty of January 7, 1935, which brought a reconciliation of the two traditional foes at Ethiopia's expense. Coming at a strategic moment, the interval between French hegemony and German military reassertion, this treaty illustrated the dilemma of France. She felt in bitter need of Italy's friendship in view of threatening Nazism. She was equally anxious to keep Britain's continuous alliance for the very same reason. The result was her diplomatic tightrope of the mid-thirties. France was not alone in the unheroic dodging of the real issues. At times it looked as if all politics around Ethiopia was nothing but a futile attempt at saving the face of the "great statesmen," Mussolini, Baldwin, Hoare, and — the two faces of Laval.

Laval was in more than one way the typical figure of the crisis. His demonic role in France's darkest hour made people forget what a significant and fateful part he had already played in the preliminaries of the disaster. In fact, he personified the basic moral default of the era that hoped to back out of the inevitable conflict by bargaining. Laval was shrewd and practical and unprincipled in his drive for power. He had won a doubtful reputation in French politics as a sly go-between, master of intrigues, and whisperer in the Chamber's corners. His parliamentarian career had led him quickly from the very left to the rightist reaction, and still made him play with sympathies of French radicalism. He was a suspicious character, no doubt; as a bon mot put it drastically: A man who spells his name from the right to the left the same way as from the left to the right cannot be trusted. Said Briand: "Alas, it is impossible to agree with everyone *and* Mr. Laval!"

Still, there was direction in Laval's plans. Abandoned was the traditional French line of collective security and grand alliances — broken by the shots at Marseilles (October 1934) that killed Foreign Minister Barthou, whose successor Laval was. He in turn wanted to establish a Latin bloc against Germanic expansion, and he was ready to pay a price for it, especially if another power, and a small one at that, had to make the sacrifice. This was at the base of his deal with Mussolini which gave Il Duce the green light for his aggression in Ethiopia — at least he thought so.

Ethiopia was not a rich prize, yet it was all that was left of Africa, whose spoils had been distributed before Italy entered the race for colonies. Besides, this only independent native state was situated between the Italian possessions Somaliland and Eritrea, and would round out Italy's empire. There were even rumors that it possessed unexplored mineral riches.

Italy had once before made her try and had not forgotten that humiliating defeat almost forty years ago. Revenge has always proved a popular motive for conquest. To wipe out the "shame of Adowa" was a precious tom-tom for Mussolini's insatiable drive for prestige. His dream, unfulfilled, was to surpass the great empire builders: Rhodes and Lyautey, and the Roman emperors Augustus and Trajan. Possession of colonies was still regarded the symbol of power. It was more thirst for status than hunger for bread that set Mussolini on his East African adventure, though he hastened to add that population pressure and dearth of raw materials forced the have-not nation into expansion.

By 1935 Italy's economic plight was indeed serious — and more so than that of any other European nation, partly owing to Italy's inherent weaknesses, partly to the regime's own measures. Diversion from internal difficulties to the glory of conquest, promising also welcome employment for millions of soldiers and war workers, became the dictatorial fashion of settling the economic crisis.

All these motives for Fascist aggression were covered up by the grandiose formula of Mussolini's mission to extend the "domain of civilization at barbarians' expense." He was to save the savage blackamoors — with the help of machine guns and airplanes, to be sure — the same people whose acceptance into the League had been sponsored by Fascist Italy in 1923.

A ready border incident at Walwal (December 1934) gave Italy the proper excuse for the staging of a mere "colonial operation." It was all too reminiscent of a Chinese incident. It also made the victim of aggression appeal to the League of Nations, and again action was suspended partly owing to Italian delaying techniques, partly to the slow-moving machinery of Geneva. After ten months of intensive troop concentration under the eyes of the British at Suez, Italy invaded in full strength the Empire of the Negus.

The campaign itself did not start off with the smashing victory that the Fascists had led the world to expect. While they naturally overcame the militarily inferior tribesmen wherever they encountered them, for months the bulk of the Ethiopian Army remained intact. And Western armchair strategists soon decreed that this colonial expedition would be swamped by the "rainy season," especially if the torrents should set in a little bit earlier than usual. From then on it was natural for democratic onlookers to count vainly on nature's miracles when the powers' resistance was wanting to hold back the aggressor. As later on in Poland, nature proved to be equally unreliable. The Italian Army, with a shift of the military command from Fascist General de Bono to Italy's renowned Marshal Badoglio, finally reached the strategic railway and broke the Ethiopian resistance in May 1936 before the rains came.

Haile Selassie, easily the most distinguished figure in the tragedy and dignified even in defeat, became the first royal exile in London, and many more were to follow.

Historical justice willed it that he was also the first to return and one of the few to keep his throne through adversity. Thus closes the circle of Ethiopia's fall and rise, but her story was by no means self-contained, as Arnold Toynbee so rightly pointed out. It was a crucial chapter, if not the turning point, in international affairs of the interwar period. It was the great test case of the League and the great powers.

To the surprise of Mussolini, Geneva promptly acted when Italian forces finally crossed the river Mareb and opened a full-fledged campaign against another League member (October 3, 1935). While there was great enthusiasm among the small nations and Great Britain for economic sanctions, the great powers did not dare to apply oil sanctions, which alone would have been fatal to Fascist aggressions.

The United States' "moral embargo" and her limitation of oil exports was a sham because it hit Ethiopia more than Italy. This was the beginning of a policy of "neutrality" which, in fact, was helping the aggressor and not the victim.

The policies of the great powers during that time revealed two serious failures of the era: a complete misreading of the war's deeper causations, and a futile escape from world responsibilities.

This was the time when the myth of the munition makers was flourishing. By no mere accident, Gerald P. Nye, die-hard isolationist, became the fierce chairman of a special Senate investigation committee that blamed all the trouble on the "merchants of death" and on the conspiracy of the international financiers. It sounded so progressive, almost radical, and was in line with the stigma given to the bankers since the great depression. The effect of Nye's "findings" was reflected in the Gallup polls when 70 per cent of those questioned affirmed that "it was a mistake of the United States to have entered the World War." The house of Morgan and Sir Basil Zaharoff, the Greek munition trader, became the villains and great mystery men of world affairs.

The result was neutrality legislation that meant to prevent American involvement by abstaining from various acts which had allegedly drawn this nation into the last war. These were the rules laid down by the lawmakers in the crucial years of 1935–37. No shipment of munitions to the belligerents, no trade with them (save on the cash-and-carry basis), no loans for them, no export to them on American ships, no American travel permit for war zones. It all added up to a free pass for the aggressor, assurance of American nonintervention in behalf of the dictator's victims.

The only alibi for this retreat from reality was the fact that the European nations, so much closer to the conflict, were no less blind to the aggressor's systematic advance.

Such incredible misjudgment largely derived from the prevailing attitude of the time. Nobody wanted to be his brother's keeper, and the "solid citizen" everywhere had only one ambition: to keep out of trouble. That is why he acquiesced in the rise of fascism within and without. Thus the quiet and the meek and the confused helped prepare the road to war in these days of careless sleepwalking.

This was also the time of sincere, though naïve, pacifism that became against its own will the handmaiden of isolationism at home and dictatorial aggression abroad. The Peace-Pledge Union of Canon Dick Sheppard mustered seven thousand enthusiasts in London's Albert Hall in June 1935, and soon found more than one hundred thousand signers. Students at Oxford and all over the Anglo-American world were promising themselves that they would not fight for "King, country, and economic imperialism"; and all that while Mussolini prepared the attack before their own eyes. Incidentally, Laval also called himself a passionate pacifist. In the name of peace he was later on to sell out France to Nazi Germany. Rudolf Hess was a "pacifist," too; of course, provided that the world would be handed over to Hitler for safekeeping. It all proved how mixed up had become the world's state of mind.

Looking back, one sees that the blame for this confusion falls more on the leaders than on the people. In fact, the Italo-Ethiopian War marked a milestone in the evolution of public opinion, which often proved to be more sincere and more advanced in realizing the issues, dangers, and necessary decisions than were the statesmen. This was especially true in Great Britain and became evident in three test cases: the Peace Ballot, the parliamentary elections, and the Hoare-Laval agreement.

The Peace Ballot of 1935, a private enterprise arranged by the League of Nations Union and a triumph for its president, Lord Cecil, was impressive not only in its unique mobilization of 11.5 million votes (i.e., 38 per cent of the total British vote!), but even more so in its unswerving confidence in the League (22:1), and the use of economic sanctions against aggressor nations (6:1). Even military sanctions were accepted by the majority though opposed by a significant minority (3:2). This popular demonstration forced the reluctant government to reverse its League policy and to accept "collective security" as its platform.

With such a popular slogan, the national government fought the elections of November 1935 and won overwhelmingly. When it turned its back on its promises to regard the "League of Nations as the keystone of British foreign policy" and accepted the "Hoare-Laval peace plan" — de facto turning Ethiopia into an Italian protectorate — a storm of popular indignation forced Baldwin again to capitulate. Sir Samuel Hoare made the scapegoat, had to make room for Anthony Eden, stanch defender of the League. It was the third victory of the people's pressure — and a promise for the future.

During this crisis public opinion had shown more common sense, healthy moral instincts, and strength of conviction than had the leaders. The people were growing up fast, yet they were still adolescent and in bitter need of guidance. More than ever did they need leaders — not tired old men who had lost the beliefs of their youth, if they ever had any, but the virile and experienced, the courageous who made articulate the alternatives, clarified the consequences of a taken stand, and thus presented a policy of the possible. This the democratic statesmen did not do. Unwillingly they followed the vague demands of their nation. They did not teach the people that there was a price to be paid for peace as well as for war, by force if necessary. If the people backed collective security, they had also to accept the risk of waging war against aggression. Instead they voted for sanctions and disarmament, in the same breath.

The leaders themselves were afraid of taking risks. The admirals were afraid of a much-talked-of Italian air force, and the politicians were afraid of the spector of communism, suspected in the shadow of a Fascist defeat. And between these fears, Mussolini bluffed his way to easy victory. On May 9, 1936, the King of Italy was proclaimed emperor of Abyssinia. On June 10 Neville Chamberlain, breaking the British cabinet's long silence, called for the withdrawal of "the policy of sanctions . . . the very midsummer of madness."

This was a declaration of the League's defeat. It brought the British government back to the position expressed on October 8, 1935, by the leading Conservative, Mr. Amery (whose son, John, was to join the services of Mr. Goebbels as a Quisling broadcaster during the Second World War). Said he: "I am not prepared to send a single Birmingham boy to his death for the sake of Abyssinia." Yet it was not Abyssinia that was at stake, but the peace of the world, the lad from Birmingham included. Lord Cecil prophetically warned in a letter to the *Times:* "We cannot escape war by running away from it. There is no escape from blackmail by submission." Still, the government succeeded in frightening the people with the horrors of war into a policy of peace at any price. There was no more direct way to the wars of the dictators.

While the Ethiopian War revealed the most serious symptoms of the world's moral malady, its repercussions became even more significant. "Italy against the world" had succeeded. The prestige of Mussolini was enhanced with his people, and the Western democracies suffered an irreparable blow.

The real winner in the Italo-Ethiopian War was Nazi Germany. The mere fact that it did not participate in the League's sanctions meant not only good business for the Reich, but also bound Italy in vassalage to Hitler. He conquered the whole Danube basin, the proud domain of Fascist control, on the battlefields of Ethiopia. This fact was soon to become clear in the Austrian episode.

The African campaign had an even more immediate effect on Germany's western frontiers. While Britain and France were fully taken up with Italy's attack, Hitler seized the strategic opportunity to remilitarize the Rhineland (March 7, 1936). It was not Germany's first breach of the Versailles Treaty. It had been preceded by Hitler's surprise move of general conscription (March 16, 1935).

His next bold stroke was the end of Locarno, called off by Hitler under the flimsy pretext that the Franco-Russian Treaty (May 1935) had deprived Locarno of its "inner meaning." Alas, it had been lost with Hitler's rise to power. The march into the Rhineland broke the real defense line between two political eras. With the West Wall fortifications erected, French military aid for southeastern Europe was definitely blocked. It was the end of the sanitary cordon around Germany, and it was the strategic end of the Succession States, too. It was the beginning of Hitler's march down the Danube.

This was all an extension of Mussolini's "colonial operation," yet before Hitler collected his spoils in central Europe, the world's attention was drawn to the periphery of the Continent. As if fate wanted to give the Führer more time for careful plotting and preparation! Or was it, after Manchuria and Ethiopia, a third and final chance for the powers' awakening? If the Spanish Civil War could not arouse them, only war in earnest could; for Spain was the great dress rehearsal.

GERMANY AND THE ATTACK
UPON ABYSSINIA

ELIZABETH WISKEMANN

Hitler started as the embarrassed suitor of Mussolini, but Mussolini ended as Hitler's cipher, and the Axis was motivated by Hitler. Thus writes Elizabeth Wiskemann, presently professor of international relations at the University of Edinburgh, author of numerous books and frequent contributor on German, Central and Eastern European affairs to leading journals in Great Britain and the United States. The Ethiopian Crisis served as the crucial lever in this reversal of roles. The anti-German alignment, symbolized by the Stresa meeting of French, British, and Italians in April 1935 to protest the German repudiation of the armament clauses of the Treaty of Versailles, shifted by October of the following year to the formal establishment of the Rome-Berlin Axis. The question posed by Miss Wiskemann is whether this alliance came about as the result of clever machinations by the German dictator or was due to a tragic lack of coordination between the democracies, Britain and France.

DIPLOMATS who worked for many years with Mussolini believe that he always yearned after an alliance with France, about which, in his completely different way, he had some of Hitler's feelings about Britain. After the murder of Dollfuss, while he obviously enjoyed the prestige he was winning as the protector of Europe and the champion of civilized values, he several times threw out the hint that Italy could not always be the only Power to mobilize against Hitler. The 25 July 1934 had in fact brought about a small-scale *rapprochment* between Italy and the Western Powers in Vienna, where the three Chargés d'Affaires (in the absence of their Ministers, who were away on holiday) spent the days and nights from 25 July to 28 July together. The Little Entente representatives, incidentally, did much the same, watching the three Chargés of the Great Powers nervously.

In Fascist eyes Czechoslovakia, Yugoslavia, and Rumania were nothing but the lackeys of France. The relations between Fascist Italy and the Powers joined in the Little Entente were also conditioned in a general way by Mussolini's revisionism and encouragement to Hungary, and more specifically by the anger which his support of Croat separatism engendered at Belgrade. The leading *Ustaša* or Croat terrorist, Ante Pavelić, who also had connexions with the I.M.R.O., the Macedonian terrorist organization, had left Yugoslavia in 1929 and spent the intervening five years in Italy and Hungary, and occasionally in Austria and Germany. The Croats were traditionally the most *kaisertreu* of the former Austrian Slavs, and their quarrel with the Serbs fortified the fierce Serb hatred of the Habsburg dynasty. This united Czechs and Serbs and made the Little Entente fanatically hostile to the possibilities of any kind

From Elizabeth Wiskemann, *The Rome-Berlin Axis* (New York, 1949), pp. 41–52. Reprinted by permission of the Oxford University Press.

of Habsburg restoration. For years these feelings gave the arch-hater of the Habsburgs, Adolf Hitler, a useful weapon in dealing with his future victims of the Little Entente, not excepting Dr. Beneš. Göring's visit to Yugoslavia earlier in 1934 had strengthened the Serbs in the belief that the Anschluss might be the best veto on a restoration, at which, as the Nazis always insinuated, Dollfuss and the Clericals — both Austrian and Italian — were aiming. At the same time, of course, the Nazis flirted with Croats and Macedonians — disruptive elements might be useful anywhere. Rosenberg, who was, roughly speaking, Hitler's agent for the disruption of Russia, though he never stooped to the racial depths of Latin questions, patronized all kinds of Slavs, including a group in Berlin called the "Croatia-Presse."

At the time of Dollfuss's murder it seemed as if war might be provoked, not directly between Italy and Germany but rather between Italy and Yugoslavia. The Yugoslavs were frightened of the Italians on their weak northern frontier, and on the other hand it was, perhaps, only a *démenti* of news that Yugoslav troops had entered Austria which prevented the Alpini from crossing the Brenner. Many Austrian Nazis subsequently took refuge in Maribor (Marburg), in Slovenia. On 9 October the Adriatic air became heavier still with the murder at Marseilles of Alexander of Yugoslavia together with the French Foreign Minister, Barthou, by a Macedonian terrorist. Now Mussolini at that time had no interest in the perpetration of this crime, which may have been engineered at the last moment by no higher authority than the I.M.R.O. and the *Ustaši;* certainly it served no one's purpose except that of the Germans. Though the terrorist Göring assured the Yugoslav journalists at Belgrade on 17 October that the Reich countenanced no terrorists, on 27 October he admitted to François-Poncet, as did Neurath on the 24th, that Rosenberg had been "careless." Clues implicated Pavelić and his fellow-conspirator, Kvaternik, who were arrested

in Turin on 18 October, and it was subsequently discovered that Pavelić had left Berlin for Milan very suddenly on the eve of the murder. François-Poncet himself experienced the difficulties made by the Germans, when, after many warm offers from them, a representative of the Sûreté Nationale came to Berlin to investigate. Meanwhile Mussolini refused the extradition of Pavelić and Kvaternik, and it was tacitly agreed that Yugoslavia should vent her anger against Hungary as the protector of assassins. It took several months for the rage of Yugoslavia to subside.

Barthou had been intending to proceed to Rome, and Mussolini had already prepared to welcome him in his speech in Milan on 6 October, when he warned Germany that she should not "estrange herself from Europe's historical evolution," and spoke with enthusiasm of his hope of an understanding with France. It was finally with Laval in January 1935 that a Franco-Italian agreement was signed. After the noisy speeches of many years, Italy showed herself astonishingly yielding in the matters of territorial readjustments in Africa and the status of Italians in Tunisia; a few faintly practical steps for the international defence of Austria were planned. In February an Italo-Austrian Cultural Agreement was signed, and shortly afterwards the Italian *Capo* himself contributed a rather trite article to the *Popolo d'Italia* on the "Historic Mission of Austria," which he defined more or less as that of a clearing-house for Italian artists. He laid great emphasis upon the catholicism of Austria, and concluded with the importance of Austria's community of language with Germany and of religion with Italy. The German return to conscription on 16 March did nothing to lessen Mussolini's expressions of wrath against northern barbarism and led to a fresh Franco-Italian encounter, to which the British were invited, at Stresa in April. Both at Rome in January and at Stresa in April Mussolini showed the technical incompetence as a negotiator of a man who was little but an orator and a journalist.

He lacked the legal training of higher Italian functionaries, and where Hitler deliberately generated clouds of confusion by his interminable speeches, Mussolini, even before his young son-in-law, Count Ciano, took charge of the Palazzo Chigi, created confusion through sheer amateurishness. Others who were concerned with the Franco-Italian agreement consider that Laval was well aware that Mussolini was being generous in the hope of gaining liberty of action in Ethiopia, but Laval imagined that there would be no breach of the peace — the Italians would proceed as the French had in Morocco a generation earlier; Laval was certainly speaking the truth when he afterwards insisted that he had never agreed in any form to an open attack on Ethiopia. At Stresa there was a tremendous gathering of diplomats and journalists. A succulent lunch at the Isola dei Pescatori brought together the respective specialists on Ethiopia, including the Foreign Office representative, Mr. Maurice Peterson, and while the greatest cordiality reigned and agreement about obvious Ethiopian technicalities was expressed, the possibility of *action* in Ethiopia was never mentioned. The result was that Mussolini became convinced that both France and Britain were willing for him to annex Ethiopia as it might please him, in return for his services against Germany. Ciano echoed the Duce's phrases about civilized man and northern barbarism when, as Minister of Propaganda, he opened the exhibition of Italian painting in Paris. And if Britain were still in doubt it was Ciano who received Lord Tyrrell at his country-house in August, and, when asked what Italy really wanted, replied without hesitation, "But we want Ethiopia."

At French instigation an Italian-Yugoslav *détente* had been initiated when a new Italian Minister arrived in Belgrade in March. This gave substance to the project of an Italian-led south-eastern Europe, and when in May 1935 the Franco-Russian and Czech-Russian treaties were signed the solidarity of the Continent against Hitler

seemed complete. Great Britain's White Paper early in March had drawn attention to certain obvious dangers in National Socialism, but at Stresa Sir John Simon was cool about Austrian integrity. Suddenly the solidarity of Europe was shaken in June by the — as it seemed to the Continent — inexplicable defection of Britain, and the Anglo-German naval treaty created a breach in the wall of Germany's isolation.

Thus during the first half of 1935 the relations between Mussolini and Hitler were as bad as they could be. The Polish Ambassador, Lipski, was something of an *homme de confiance* to the German régime, since the German-Polish Agreement of 1934 had brought Hitler this one strange friendship; he had a talk with Göring at the Schorfheide at the end of April 1935, when Göring complained bitterly that Mussolini was working against Germany in every possible field. At the beginning of May Lipski saw Göring again; the latter was still angry. He grumbled that, as they had told Mussolini at the time, Germany had only come into the Four-Power Pact to please the Duce and this was Germany's reward. . . . Like nearly all Göring's frank confidences, this was untrue; it has been seen that Germany had joined the Pact of June 1933 because her Minister of War had chosen to do so.

After the assassination of Dollfuss, the Austrian Government and State had been patched together somehow and even attained a certain appearance of solidarity for the next couple of years. The Clericals, through the President of the Austrian State, Miklas, insisted upon Schuschnigg as successor to Dollfuss, with Starhemberg still as Vice-Chancellor; since Schuschnigg was far less flexible than Dollfuss, the new Clerical-Heimwehr coalition was difficult from the start, and since Schuschnigg was known in principle to desire a Habsburg restoration, it gave, as one or two clear-sighted individuals at once perceived, marvellous opportunities to Franz von Papen. This political harlequin has been seen to have been instrumental in bringing Hitler into power in Germany, and then into the presence of his chosen Master at Venice on 14 June. Three days later Papen delivered his famous Marburg speech written for him by the unfortunate Edgar Jung in any thing but a Nazi spirit. Everyone thought for a moment that Germany was returning to her senses, only to learn that Jung had been among the hundreds murdered by Hitler's orders on 30 June, while Papen, after one of his habitual thriller-escapes, blandly accepted the murder of his personal secretary and other of his associates: what was more, he also accepted the post of Hitler's special envoy to Vienna on the day after the murder of Dollfuss. The Italians were not amused and insisted that Miklas should delay the *agrément* at least until after the funeral of Dollfuss on 29 July.

Until the autumn of 1935 a certain stability was maintained in Austria. Schuschnigg had quickly found occasion to visit the Duce to establish personal contact. His stiff ascetic personality and his Tyrolese associations did not please Mussolini; the Duce, however, arranged to keep in direct touch with him through Senator Salata, a Triestino who was director of the Italian Institute in Vienna, and who had intervened, against the wishes of the Italian Legation there, to bring about the Duce's acquiescence in Papen's special mission. For his dealings with Starhemberg Mussolini still used Morreale, who was on the worst of terms with Salata.

For the moment Austria profited economically from the political situation. During the summer of 1935 there were enough other tourists to make up for the Germans who had for two years been kept north of the frontier by the 1,000-mark tax demanded by the Reich Government from those of them who wished to cross it. The Rome Protocols served Austria well, various exports to Italy increasing, and the expansion of Italy's Danubian horizon created a strong Italian interest in the Danube Shipping Company. Above all, Italian preparations for an attack on Ethiopia kept the Hirtenberg arms factory in Austria fully employed.

For a year Papen made no progress. On 27 July he, or some more intelligent member of his staff, wrote an important dispatch to Berlin which deserves a good deal of quotation. It begins by referring to the general hostility to Germany caused by the Austrian question. Every German effort in a southeastern direction will run up against this opposition, especially since Italy regards the Danube basin as her *Expansionsgebiet*. As between Germany and Austria Papen absolutely condemns the Habicht type of open terrorism which had culminated in the Dollfuss crime. Austria is now based upon militant Catholicism and a Heimwehr which is "enthusiastically favourable to Mussolini." "The dream of resurrecting the Holy Roman Empire around Vienna becomes more grotesque the more this idea of the Austrian imperialist romantics is exploited by Mussolini in order to advance his conception of a new *imperium romanum* at the expense of the German nation." We must, continues Papen, create a mission of the united Germans to triumph over the idea of an Austrian mission, and we must insist that our mission, if opposed to political Catholicism, in no way undermines the fundamental Christianity of Germany. It was Papen who had negotiated Hitler's Concordat with the Vatican in July 1933 — that first external concession to Hitler, as Pechel emphasizes — and it was mainly on account of his Catholic connexions that Hitler had sent him to Vienna. Mussolini was only too well aware, as he said to Starhemberg, that Papen, with his astonishing ability to make everyone feel he was their particular friend, was more dangerous than Habicht.

All this time, far from finding the champions of the Austrians in South Tyrol mere drivellers, Adolf Hitler found them all too useful. In vain did Mussolini and Dollfuss or Schuschnigg try to emphasize that the Italian authorities were being more conciliatory on account of the Rome-Vienna friendship; the young Tyrolese, whether of Innsbruck or Bolzano, were convinced that Hitler had dictated terms at Venice or at some point later. The Bavarian Press was allowed to be extremely violent about Italian oppression, which had been drastic; but without any particular justification the wicked Latins were attacked in the winter of 1934–5 for suppressing noble Nordic Christmas-trees. It was easy to whip up feeling against Italy in Germany, and of course in Austria and South Tyrol, and at the end of April 1935 the *Münchner Neueste Nachrichten* — the leading newspaper of Munich — was banned in Italy.

The German Press was also clearly hostile to Italy in the matter of her East African policy, and an Ufa film called *Abessinien von Heute*, which was markedly friendly to the Negus and his rule, was shown all over Germany during this spring (1935). In June there was a passing, if prophetic, rumour of an Italian-German deal, Italy to drop Austria and Germany to back her over Abyssinia, but the Germans' pose, and indeed their only hope just then after the Naval Agreement, was to be Britain's friend and as such opposed to Italy. This was in fact the policy of the German Foreign Office and the Naval Staff, as also of the Reichswehr, which despised the Italian Army and expected a fresh Italian fiasco in Abyssinia. The Nazi Party felt confused between its contempt for racial inferiors and the defenders of Austrian "separatism," and its hatred of the League of Nations and the *status quo*. In northern Germany hatred of Italy on account of the so-called treachery of 1915 and the South Tyrol was a little less intense than in the south; especially at this time the feeling about Danzig was stronger and therefore perhaps also the feeling against Geneva. Until it was clear that Mussolini's Abyssinian policy would bring him into conflict with the League, it enjoyed no sympathy in Germany.

In Hitler's mind, however, no breach with Mussolini occurred, and there were one or two individuals whose interests urged them to encourage this belief. Baron Braun von Stumm held an important position in the Press Department of the German Foreign Office; his second wife was a highly neurotic Italian woman, Giuseppina Antinori. Probably before the end of 1934 she and Ciano's sister, who was Countess Magistrati, met Hitler secretly without the knowledge of Cerruti, to try to counteract external tendencies. The Braun von Stumm household was in every sense an Italo-German meeting-ground; it was here, for instance, that Professor Manacorda of Florence University was often received. He was both ultra-Fascist and ultra-Catholic, and on his journeys to Germany (which began in 1936) he gave himself the airs of an important intermediary between the Vatican, Italy, and Germany. But, though he occasionally saw the Pope and the Duce and the Führer, it is unlikely that he affected the trend of their relations perceptibly.

At the beginning of August 1935, on account of the Danzig-League of Nations crisis, Lipski visited Hitler at Berchtesgaden. With a certain regret the Führer remarked that his path had diverged from that of Mussolini on acount of Austria. Mussolini had failed to understand the situation, and he was now taking a grave risk in provoking the other Powers over Abyssinia. But, added Hitler, though the Duce was hostile to Germany he would regard a defeat of Mussolini as a disaster, because it would constitute too great a blow to their common Fascist-Nazi ideology. It was always the same thing. Hitler knew. Anyone who did not accept his view did not understand. And Mussolini never really knew — until perhaps on the shores of Garda in 1944 — that Hitler had cast him for partner in his own Satanic revolution.

At all events it was clear to Lipski that Hitler was already determined, whatever Neurath and the German Foreign Office might wish, to prevent the humiliation of Mussolini. And, as always seemed to happen in that fatal decade, events so played into Hitler's hands that when he spoke in March 1936 of his *Schlafwandlerische Sicherheit* it was difficult not to be impressed. Already by the end of June 1935, without evidence (beyond Schacht's general policy) of any German scheming to bring it about, Italy had become the leading buyer of German coal. By now Cerruti was scarcely on speaking-terms with the Wilhelmstrasse and still less with Hitler. Mussolini decided to move Cerruti to Paris and to bring Attolico, his Ambassador in Moscow, to Berlin. At this point occurred one of history's ironies. Attolico, the man who four years later kept Italy out of the war, was so anxious in August 1935 to start his mission well that he would not wait till Hitler's return to Berlin in September in order to present his credentials. It was arranged that Hitler should come from Berchtesgaden to Berlin at the end of August for this purpose, and in consequence Attolico was bound to go to the Nazi Party Congress in September 1935, although in 1934 no Italian diplomat had attended it. This was not, of course, without the approval of the Duce, who had shown signs of anxiety about his relations with Germany since June; at this time a breakdown in the League negotiations over the Abyssinian controversy was becoming apparent.

In October Mussolini attacked Ethiopia, which he could probably have had without firing a shot. It is interesting that several leading Fascists told Starhemberg that they were opposed to the venture. But Mussolini's was a journalistic determination to fight at all costs as a demonstration of force, because purely political action might be too "decadent" to impress that self-same Hitler, who never wasted superfluous force upon the acquisition of power. The outbreak of war in Abyssinia was followed by a superficial strengthening of the Duce's position in Austria. While Schuschnigg remained Chancellor, Starhemberg on 17 October got rid of Fey, who had been undermining the Heimwehr in Hitler's interest, and took over the Ministry of the Interior for himself; at the same time he put at the head of the Austrian Ministry of Finance Draxler, hitherto legal adviser to Starhem-

berg's friend, the arms manufacturer Mandl, who, according to Papen, inspired Starhemberg with all his own Jewish *ressentiment* against Hitler. Mandl was the owner of Hirtenberg and of arms factories in Italy, and as unpleasant as arms manufacturers are traditionally said to be. It was a most valuable asset to the Nazi cause that Austrian policy could now be interpreted as subordinate to Herr Mandl's desire for profit. "How far Italian pressure affected Starhemberg . . . cannot be exactly gauged. But I learn on good authority that Mussolini urgently demanded a strengthening of the authority of the Austrian Government"; Papen had also heard that Starhemberg was convinced that Italy's venture would succeed. The German Minister in Vienna was quick enough to sense that the Austrian Italophiles had overreached themselves. The unpopularity of Italy was now reinforced in Austria by dislike of being identified with Mussolini's defiance of Geneva and by anxiety as to the defence of Austria if the Italian Army were busy in East Africa. People complained that Austria had been led into a cul-de-sac; she now depended *einzig und allein* upon the victory of Mussolini.

A week or so later it was the talk of Vienna that Herr von Papen's car had been left several times, gaily and indiscreetly flying its swastika flag, outside the office of the Clerical and semi-official newspaper, the *Reichspost*. It was here that together with its editor, Dr. Funder, he now began to plan the Press Agreement of the following July. Funder seems to have been perfectly genuine; it is all the more surprising that he should have been willing to discuss with Papen at this time not only an agreement about the Press, but also the question of the Austrian Nazis who had become Austrian Legionaries in the Reich and were being trained for a *coup*. He actually told Papen, if the latter may be believed, that he favoured a secret agreement because there were so many people both within Austria and without who were interested in preventing an Austro-German agreement. The acceptance by Mussolini of the Press Agreement which emerged later on may be regarded as the occasion of the birth of the Axis friendship; it was made possible by Mussolini's weakness, and because he was weak it was certain to spell the end of Austrian independence.

When Mussolini visited Berlin in September 1937 he spoke of the autumn of 1935 as the period of the birth of the Axis, but all this time the atmosphere around the Italian Embassy in Berlin was, Attolico notwithstanding, extremely cool. The Reich Government forbad the export of arms to either belligerent, so Attolico concentrated his energy on procuring coal and other raw materials from Germany, but even over supplies such as these the Germans were not encouraging. In October German exporters were warned to be cautious towards Italy in view of the large accumulation of lira balances awaiting transfer, and at the beginning of November the Reich declared an embargo upon the export of oils, fats, textiles, potatoes, iron, and steel, but not coal. On 7 November, soon after the League Sanctions decision, when Austria and Hungary voted with Italy, the *Deutsches Nachrichten Büro* issued the following statement:

The German standpoint with reference to Germany's neutrality is well known and has in no way altered. Should an abnormal increase of exports of raw materials or foodstuffs become apparent, which threatens Germany's own economic interests, the German Government will prevent it by appropriate measures.

If Neurath in conversation with foreign diplomats showed a slightly pro-Italian inclination, the line he followed was that, between Italy and the League, Germany was absolutely neutral. In Papen's already quoted dispatch of July he had written:

It might be possible that through the menace to British imperial interests the Abyssinian adventure would help to bring nearer the realisation of the New Order. It remains more probable, however, that a compromise will be made at the Negus's expense — at the cost perhaps also of a notable blood-letting of Italy.

Indeed, the possibility of this compromise tormented Hitler and his Ministers during the last months of 1935; were it to be realized, Hitler feared for the programme of his life. On 9 December it seemed that the blow had fallen, for on that day the Hoare-Laval Agreement of 7 December was revealed in the French Press. Consternation reigned in Berlin at the renewed possibility of complete German isolation, and the German Press suddenly became the champion of the League of Nations against this "plot." Lipski was treated to a lecture in this vein when he visited Neurath about a week later. Two days after this he saw Hitler, who was greatly excited and asked him over and over again what on earth the British were doing. He then indulged in a long apology for Germany's exports to Italy. He was not, he insisted, profiting from the situation, but he had to consider a serious problem of unemployment in his coalmines: the French might accuse him of having placed an embargo upon the export of arms to the belligerents because he wished to stack up all possible armaments for himself, but this was unjust, for the deliveries in question would have been too trifling to affect the Reich. After speaking of other things Hitler reverted feverishly to the Hoare-Laval plan.

Mussolini was ready to accept the Franco-British proposition, and the French, who knew that if the Abyssinian war were not stopped Hitler would re-militarize the Rhineland and thereby emasculate the Treaty of Versailles, were determined to preserve the Stresa front and the isolation of Germany. The French believed, however, that the British (contrary to the popular legend) were less politically practical than themselves; some of them also knew of the instinctive anti-Latin and pro-German character of British public opinion, which to this day confuses the commonplace opportunism of Mussolini with the fearful logic of Hitler. It was therefore planned in Paris to spring the news on Baldwin, who would have difficulty in repudiating his own Foreign Secretary. The remarkable and admirable reaction of the British against the Hoare-Laval plan was all the greater, the Stresa front was dissolved, and Hitler unshackled, let loose to advance step by step, from the militarization of the Rhineland to the invasion of Poland. History has perhaps never played a stranger trick upon Man than to allow British indignation against international lawlessness and imperialist and racial bullying to have smoothed the path of Adolf Hitler. Out of this misconception was born that deformity, the Italo-German alliance, of which Hitler had so long dreamed.

THE COUNTERFEIT PEACE

ALAN BULLOCK

Beneficiary of the drift and uncertainty of the nineteen-thirties was ultimately Adolf Hitler. The cleft which developed over Ethiopia among Italy, Britain, and France was eagerly exploited by the German dictator in his course of obtaining for Germany freedom of action on the road to European hegemony. The following excerpt, taken from the excellent biography of Hitler by Alan Bullock, noted English specialist on twentieth-century Germany, brings out this interaction of clever calculation and quick utilization of fortuitous circumstance.

FROM the summer of 1934 the principal object of the Western Powers' diplomacy was to persuade Germany to sign a pact of mutual assistance covering Eastern Europe. Just as the Locarno Pact included France, Germany, Belgium, Great Britain and Italy, each undertaking to come to the immediate aid of France and Belgium, or Germany, if either side were attacked by the other, so this Eastern Locarno would include Russia, Germany, Poland, Czechoslovakia and the other states of Eastern Europe and would involve the same obligation of automatic assistance in the case of an attack.

Hitler had no intention of entering into any such scheme: it was not aggression that he feared, but checks upon his freedom of action. His preference — for obvious reasons — was for bilateral agreements, and if he were to sign a multilateral pact of non-aggression it would only be one from which all provisions for mutual aid had been removed, a statement of good intentions unsupported by any guarantees to enforce them. German opposition, which had already been made clear in 1934, was powerfully assisted by that of Poland. Pilsudski was highly suspicious of Russia and anxious that Poland should not be pushed into

the front line of an anti-German combination — which could only mean that Poland would be either the battleground of a new clash between her two neighbours or the victim of a deal concluded between them at her expense, as happened in 1939. Polish quarrels with Lithuania and dislike of Czechoslovakia added further reasons to his reluctance to enter any such all-embracing project. Pilsudski, and his successor Beck, saw the only way out of Poland's difficulties as a policy of balancing between Moscow and Berlin, a policy which fatally overestimated Poland's strength, and fatally underestimated the danger from Germany.

Hitler courted the Poles assiduously, constantly urging on them the common interest Poland and Germany had in opposing Russia. "Poland," he told the Polish Ambassador in November, 1933, "is an outpost against Asia. . . . The other States should recognize this role of Poland's."

Goering, who was used by Hitler in the role of a candid friend of the Poles, spoke even more plainly when he visited Warsaw at the end of January, 1935. He began his conversations in the Polish Foreign Ministry by mentioning the possibility of a new partition of Poland by agreement between Germany and Russia. But he did this only

From Alan Bullock *Hitler: A Study in Tyranny* (New York, 1952), pp. 301–311. Reprinted by permission of Harper and Brothers and Odhams Press Ltd.

to dismiss it as a practical impossibility: in fact, he continued, Hitler's policy needed a strong Poland, to form a common barrier with Germany against the Soviet Union. In his talks with Polish generals and with Marshal Pilsudski, Goering "outlined far-reaching plans, almost suggesting an anti-Russian alliance and a joint attack on Russia. He gave it to be understood that the Ukraine would become a Polish sphere of influence and North-western Russia would be Germany's." The Poles were wary of such seductive propositions, but they were impressed by the friendliness of the German leaders, and in the course of 1935 relations between the two governments became steadily closer. Goering visited Cracow for Pilsudski's funeral in May. The same month Hitler himself had a long conversation with the Ambassador, and after a visit of the Polish Foreign Minister, Colonel Beck, to Berlin in July the communiqué spoke of "a far-reaching agreement of views." The attention Hitler paid to Polish-German relations was to repay him handsomely.

Meanwhile, the British and French Governments renewed their attempts to reach a settlement with Germany. The Saar plebiscite in January, 1935, had produced a ninety per cent vote for the return of the territory to Germany. The result had scarcely been in doubt, although the Nazis cried it up inside Germany as a great victory and the destruction of the first of the Versailles fetters. The removal of this issue between France and Germany, which Hitler had constantly described as the one territorial issue dividing them, seemed to offer a better chance of finding the Fuehrer in a more reasonable mood.

The proposals which the British and French Ambassadors presented to Hitler at the beginning of February, 1935, sketched the outline of a general settlement which would cover the whole of Europe. The existing Locarno Pact of mutual assistance, which applied to Western Europe, was to be strengthened by the conclusion of an agreement to cover unprovoked aggression from the air. At the same time it was to be supplemented by two similar pacts of mutual assistance, one dealing with Eastern Europe, the other with Central Europe.

Hitler faced a difficult decision. German rearmament had reached a stage where further concealment would prove a hindrance. It seemed clear from their proposals that the Western Powers would be prepared to waive their objections to German rearmament in return for Germany's accession to their proposals for strengthening and extending collective security. Against that Hitler had to set his anxiety to avoid tying his hands, and his need of some dramatic stroke of foreign policy to gratify the mood of nationalist expectation in Germany which had so far received little satisfaction. On both these grounds a bold unilateral repudiation of the disarmament clauses of the Treaty of Versailles would suit him very much better than negotiations with the Western Powers, in which he would be bound to make concessions in return for French and British agreement. Could he afford to take the risk?

Hitler's first reply showed uncertainty. He welcomed the idea of extending the original Locarno Pact to include attack from the air, while remaining evasive on the question of the proposed Eastern and Danubian Pacts. The German Government invited the British to continue discussions, and a visit to Berlin by the British Foreign Minister, Sir John Simon, was arranged for 7 March. Before the visit could take place, however, on 4 March the British Government published its own plans for increased armaments, basing this on "the fact that Germany was . . . rearming openly on a large scale, despite the provisions of Part V of the Treaty of Versailles." The British White Paper went on to remark "that not only the forces, but the spirit in which the population, and especially the youth of the country, are being organized, lend colour to, and substantiate, the general feeling of insecurity which has already been incontestably generated."

Great indignation was at once expressed in Germany, and Hitler contracted a "chill" which made it necessary to postpone Sir John Simon's visit. On the 9th the German Government officially notified foreign governments that a German Air Force was already in existence. This seems to have been a kite with which to test the Western Powers' reaction. As Sir John Simon told the House of Commons that he and Mr. Eden were still proposing to go to Berlin and nothing else happened, it appeared safe to risk a more sensational announcement the next week-end. On 16 March, 1935, the German Government proclaimed its intention of re-introducing conscription and building up a peacetime army of thirty-six divisions, with a numerical strength of five hundred and fifty thousand men.

Four days before, the French Government had doubled the period of service and reduced the age of enlistment in the French Army, in order to make good the fall in the number of conscripts due to the reduced birth-rate of the years 1914–1918. This served Hitler as a pretext for his own action. He was able to represent Germany as driven reluctantly to take this step, purely in order to defend herself against the warlike threats of her neighbours. From the time when the German people, trusting in the assurances of Wilson's Fourteen Points, and believing they were rendering a great service to mankind, had laid down their arms, they had been deceived again and again in their hopes of justice and their faith in the good intentions of others. Germany, Hitler declared, was the one Power which had disarmed; now that the other Powers, far from disarming themselves, were actually beginning to increase their armaments, she had no option but to follow suit.

The announcement was received with enthusiasm in Germany, and on 17 March, Heroes Memorial Day (*Heldengedenktag*), a brilliant military ceremony in the State Opera House celebrated the rebirth of the German Army. At Hitler's side sat von Mackensen, the only surviving field-marshal of the old Army. Afterwards, amid cheering crowds, Hitler held a review of the new Army, including a detachment of the Air Force. So widespread was German feeling against the Treaty of Versailles, and so strong the pride in the German military tradition, that German satisfaction at the announcement could be taken for granted. Everything turned on the reaction abroad to this first open breach of the Treaty's provisions. Hitler had anticipated protests, and was prepared to discount them; what mattered was the action with which the other signatories of the Treaty proposed to support their protests.

The result more than justified the risks he had taken. The British Government, after making a solemn protest, proceeded to ask whether the Fuehrer was still ready to receive Sir John Simon. The French appealed to the League, and an extraordinary session of the Council was at once summoned, to be preceded by a conference between Great Britain, France and Italy at Stresa. But the French Note, too, spoke of searching for means of conciliation and of the need to dispel the tension which had arisen. This was not the language of men who intended to enforce their protests. When Sir John Simon and Mr. Eden at last visited Berlin at the end of March they found Hitler polite, even charming, but perfectly sure of himself and firm in his refusal to consider any pact of mutual assistance which included the Soviet Union. He made a good deal of the service Germany was performing in safeguarding Europe against Communism, and, when the discussion moved to German rearmament, asked: "Did Wellington, when Blücher came to his assistance at Waterloo, first ask the legal experts of the Foreign Office whether the strength of the Prussian forces exceeded the limits fixed by treaty?" It was the Englishmen who had come to ask for co-operation and Hitler who was in the advantageous position of being able to say "no," without having anything to ask in return. The very presence of the British representatives in Berlin, after the announcement of 16 March, was a triumph for his diplomacy.

In the weeks that followed, the Western Powers continued to make a display of European unity which, formally at least, was more impressive. At Stresa, on 11 April, the British, French and Italian Governments condemned Germany's action, reaffirmed their loyalty to the Locarno Treaty and repeated their declaration on Austrian independence. At Geneva the Council of the League duly censured Germany and appointed a committee to consider what steps should be taken the next time any State endangered peace by repudiating its obligations. Finally, in May, the French Government, having failed to make headway with its plan for a general treaty of mutual assistance in Eastern Europe, signed a pact with the Soviet Union by which each party undertook to come to the aid of the other in case of an unprovoked attack. This treaty was flanked by a similar pact, concluded at the same time, between Russia and France's most reliable ally, Czechoslovakia.

Yet, even if Hitler was taken aback by the strength of this belated reaction, and if the Franco-Russian and Czech-Russian treaties in particular faced him with awkward new possibilities, his confidence in his own tactics was never shaken. He proceeded to test the strength of this newfound unity; it did not take long to show its weaknesses.

On 21 May Hitler appeared before the Reichstag to deliver a long and carefully prepared speech on foreign policy. It is a speech worth studying, for in it are to be found most of the tricks with which Hitler lulled the suspicions and raised the hopes of the gullible. His answer to the censure of the Powers was not defiance, but redoubled assurances of peace, an appeal to reason, justice and conscience. The new Germany, he protested, was misunderstood, and his own attitude misrepresented.

No man ever spoke with greater feeling of the horror and stupidity of war than Adolf Hitler.

The blood shed on the European continent in the course of the last three hundred years bears no proportion to the national result of the events. In the end France has remained France, Germany Germany, Poland Poland and Italy Italy. What dynastic egoism, political passion and patriotic blindness have attained in the way of apparently far-reaching political changes by shedding rivers of blood has, as regards national feeling, done no more than touched the skin of the nations. It has not substantially altered their fundamental characters. If these States had applied merely a fraction of their sacrifices to wiser purposes the success would certainly have been greater and more permanent. . . . If the nations attach so much importance to an increase in the number of the inhabitants of a country they can achieve it without tears in a simpler and more natural way. A sound social policy, by increasing the readiness of a nation to have children, can give its own people more children in a few years than the number of aliens that could be conquered and made subject to that nation by war.

Collective security, Hitler pointed out, was a Wilsonian idea, but Germany's faith in Wilsonian ideas, at least as practised by the former Allies, had been destroyed by her treatment after the war. Germany had been denied equality, had been treated as a nation with second-class rights, and driven to rearm by the failure of the other Powers to carry out their obligation to disarm. Despite this experience, Germany was still prepared to co-operate in the search for security. But she had rooted objections to the proposal of multilateral pacts, for this was the way to spread, not to localize war. Moreover, in the east of Europe, Hitler declared, there was a special case, the existence of a State, Bolshevik Russia, pledged to destroy the independence of Europe, a State with which a National Socialist Germany could never come to terms.

What Hitler offered in place of the "unrealistic" proposal of multilateral treaties was the signature of non-aggression pacts with all Germany's neighbours. The only exception he made was Lithuania, since Lithuania's continued possession of the German Memelland was a wrong which the German people could never accept, and a plain denial of that right of self-determination proclaimed by Wilson. Germany's improved relations with Poland, he did not fail to add, showed how great a contribution such pacts could make to the cause of peace: this was the practical way in which Germany set about removing international misunderstandings.

Hitler supported his offer with the most convincing display of goodwill. The fact that Germany had repudiated the disarmament clauses of the Treaty of Versailles did not mean that she had anything but the strictest regard for the Treaty's other provisions — including the demilitarization of the Rhineland — or for her other obligations under the Locarno Treaty. She had no intention of annexing Austria and was perfectly ready to strengthen the Locarno Pact by an agreement on air attack, such as Great Britain and France had suggested. She was ready to agree to the abolition of heavy arms, such as the heaviest tanks and artillery; to limit the use of other weapons — such as the bomber and poison gas — by international convention; indeed, to accept an over-all limitation of armaments provided that it was to apply to all the Powers. Hitler laid particular stress on his willingness to limit German naval power to thirty-five per cent of the strength of the British Navy. He understood very well, he declared, the special needs of the British Empire, and had no intentions of starting a new naval rivalry with Great Britain. He ended with a confession of his faith in peace. "Whoever lights the torch of war in Europe can wish for nothing but chaos. We, however, live in the firm conviction that in our time will be fulfilled, not the decline, but the renaissance of the West. That Germany may make an imperishable contribution to this great work is our proud hope and our unshakable belief."

Hitler's mastery of the language of Geneva was unequalled. His grasp of the mood of public opinion in the Western democracies was startling, considering that he had never visited any of them and spoke no foreign language. He understood intuitively their longing for peace, the idealism of the pacifists, the uneasy conscience of the liberals, the reluctance of the great mass of their peoples to look beyond their own private affairs. At this stage in the game these were greater assets than the uncompleted panzer divisions and bomber fleets he was still building, and Hitler used them with the same skill he had shown in playing on German grievances and illusions.

In *Mein Kampf* Hitler had written: "For a long time to come there will be only two Powers in Europe with which it may be possible for Germany to conclude an alliance. These Powers are Great Britain and Italy." The greatest blunder of the Kaiser's Government — prophetic words — had been to quarrel with Britain and Russia at the same time: Germany's future lay in the east, a continental future, and her natural ally was Great Britain, whose power was colonial, commercial and naval, with no territorial interests on the continent of Europe. "Only by alliance with England was it possible (before 1914) to safeguard the rear of the new German crusade. . . . No sacrifice should have been considered too great, if it was a necessary means of gaining England's friendship. Colonial and naval ambitions should have been abandoned."

Although Hitler's attitude towards Britain was modified later by growing contempt for the weakness of her policy and the credulity of her government, the idea of an alliance with her attracted him throughout his life. It was an alliance which could only, in Hitler's view, be made on condition that Britain abandoned her old balance-of-power policy in Europe, accepted the prospect of a German hegemony on the Continent and left Germany a free hand in attaining it. Even during the war Hitler persisted in believing that an alliance with

Germany on these terms was in Britain's own interests, continually expressed his regret that the British had been so stupid as not to see this, and never quite gave up the hope that he would be able to overcome their obstinacy and persuade them to accept his view. No British Government, even before the war, was prepared to go as far as an alliance on these terms, yet there was a section of British opinion which was sufficiently impressed by Hitler's arguments to be attracted to the idea of a settlement which would have left him virtually a free hand in Central and Eastern Europe, and Hitler, if he never succeeded in his main objective, was remarkably successful for a time in weakening the opposition of Great Britain to the realization of his aims. The policy of appeasement is not to be understood unless it is realized that it represented the acceptance by the British Government, at least in part, of Hitler's view of what British policy should be.

The speech of 21 May had been intended to influence opinion in Great Britain in Hitler's favour. The quickness of the British reaction was surprising. During his visit to Berlin in March Sir John Simon had been sufficiently impressed by a hint thrown out by the Fuehrer to suggest that German representatives should come to London to discuss the possibility of a naval agreement between the two countries. Hitler must have been delighted to see the speed with which the British Foreign Minister responded to his bait, and in his speech of 21 May he again underlined his willingness to arrive at such an understanding. Even Hitler, however, can scarcely have calculated that the British Government would be so maladroit as to say nothing of their intentions to the Powers with whom they had been so closely associated in censuring Germany's repudiation of the Versailles disarmament clauses in the previous weeks.

Early in June Ribbentrop, whom Hitler now began to use for special missions, flew to London. Despite the brusque and tactless way in which he refused to permit

discussion of the Fuehrer's offer, he returned with the British signature of a naval pact. This bound the Germans not to build beyond thirty-five per cent of Britain's naval strength, but it tacitly recognized Germany's right to begin naval rearmament and specifically agreed by an escape-clause that, in the construction of U-boats, Germany should have the right to build up to one hundred per cent of the submarine strength of the British Commonwealth. The affront to Britain's partners, France and Italy, both of whom were also naval powers, but neither of whom had been consulted, was open and much resented. The solidarity of the Stresa Front, the unanimity of the Powers' condemnation of German rearmament was destroyed. The British Government, in its eagerness to secure a private advantage, had given a disastrous impression of bad faith. Like Poland, but without the excuse of Poland's difficult position between Germany and Russia, Great Britain had accepted Hitler's carefully calculated offer without a thought of its ultimate consequences.

In September the Fuehrer attended the Party's rally at Nuremberg. For the first time detachments of the new German Army took part in the parade and Hitler glorified the German military tradition: "in war the nation's great defiance, in peace the splendid school of our people. It is the Army which has made men of us all, and when we looked upon the Army our faith in the future of our people was always reinforced. This old glorious Army is not dead; it only slept, and now it has arisen again in you."

Hitler's speeches throughout the rally were marked by the confidence of a man sure of his hold over the people he led. The Reichstag was summoned to Nuremberg for a special session, and Hitler presented for its unanimous approval the Nuremberg Laws directed against the Jews, first depriving Germans of Jewish blood of their citizenship, the second—the Law for the Protection of German Blood and German Honour—forbidding marriages between

Germans and Jews and the employment of German servants by Jews. These laws, Hitler declared, "repay the debt of gratitude to the movement under whose symbol (the Swastika, now adopted as the national emblem) Germany has recovered her freedom."

The same month, while Hitler at Nuremberg was making use of the power he held in Germany to gratify his hatred of the Jews, a quarrel began at Geneva which was to provide him with the opportunity to extend his power outside the German frontiers of 1914.

The alliance with Mussolini's Italy to which Hitler already looked at the time he wrote *Mein Kampf* had hitherto been prevented by Mussolini's Danubian ambitions, and the Duce's self-appointed role as the patron of Austrian independence. After the murder of Dolfuss, Mussolini had been outspoken in his dislike and contempt for the "barbarians" north of the Alps, and he had co-operated with the other Powers in their condemnation of Germany's unilateral decision to rearm. Mussolini, however, had long been contemplating a showy success for his régime in Abyssinia. It may be that he was prompted by uneasy fears that his chances of expansion in Europe would soon be reduced by the growth of German power; it may be that he was stimulated by a sense of rivalry with the German dictator; it is almost certain that he hoped to profit by French and British preoccupation with German rearmament to carry out his adventure on the cheap.

Abyssinia had appealed to the League under Article 15 of the Covenant in March. So far the dispute had been discreetly kept in the background, but in September the British Government, having just made a sensational gesture of appeasement to Germany by the Naval Treaty of June, astonished the world for the second time by taking the lead at Geneva in demanding the imposition of sanctions against Italy. She supported this by reinforcing the British Fleet in the Mediterranean. To the French, who judged that Germany, not Italy, was the greater danger to the security of Europe, the British appeared to be standing on their heads and looking at events upside down.

There was only one assumption on which British policy could be defended. If the British were prepared to support sanctions against Italy to the point of war, thereby giving to the authority of the League the backing of force which it had hitherto lacked, their action might indeed so strengthen the machinery of collective security as to put a check to any aggression, whether by Italy or Germany. The outbreak of hostilities between Italy and Abyssinia in October soon put the British intentions to the test. The course pursued by the Baldwin Government made the worst of both worlds. By insisting on the imposition of sanctions Great Britain made an enemy of Mussolini and destroyed all hope of a united front against German aggression. By her refusal to drive home the policy of sanctions, in face of Mussolini's bluster, she dealt the authority of the League as well as her own prestige a fatal blow, and destroyed all hope of finding in collective security an effective alternative to the united front of the Great Powers against German aggression.

If the British Government never meant to do more than make a show of imposing sanctions it would have done better to have followed the more cynical but more realistic policy of Laval and made a deal with Italy at the beginning. Even the Hoare-Laval Pact of December, 1935, would have been a better alternative than allowing the farce of sanctions to drag on to its inconclusive and discreditable end. For the consequences of these blunders extended much farther than Abyssinia and the Mediterranean: their ultimate beneficiary was, not Mussolini, but Hitler.

Germany at first confined herself to a policy of strict neutrality in the Abyssinian affair, but the advantages to be derived from the quarrel between Italy and the Western Powers did not escape Hitler. If Italy lost the war, that would mean the weakening of the principal barrier to German ambitions in Central and South-eastern Europe. On the other hand, if Italy proved to be successful, the prospects for Hitler were still good. His one fear was that the quarrel might be patched up by some such compromise as the Hoare-Laval Pact, and when the Polish Ambassador in Berlin saw him two days after the announcement of the terms of the Hoare-Laval Agreement he found him highly excited and alarmed at this prospect. The further development of the dispute, however, only gave him greater cause for satisfaction. Not only was Italy driven into a position of isolation, in which Mussolini was bound to look more favorably on German offers of support, but the League of Nations suffered further blows to its authority from which, after its previous failure to halt Japanese aggression, it never recovered. French confidence in England was further shaken, and the belief that Great Britain was a spent force in international politics received the most damning confirmation.

The events of 1935 thus provided an unexpected opportunity for Hitler to realize his Italian plans: as Mussolini later acknowledged, it was in the autumn of 1935 that the idea of the Rome-Berlin Axis was born. No less important was the encouragement which the feebleness of the opposition to aggression gave Hitler to pursue his policy without regard to the risks. "There was now, as it turned out," writes Mr. Churchill, "little hope of averting war or of postponing it by a trial of strength equivalent to war. Almost all that remained open to France and Britain was to await the moment of the challenge and do the best they could."

THE UNITED STATES TAKES REFUGE IN "NEUTRALITY" LEGISLATION

HERBERT FEIS

In the United States, faced with a strong current of isolationist sentiment, the policy-making agencies believed that open support of the League of Nations in the crisis would provoke heated opposition and harm the democratic cause. The cautious policy which was consequently adopted is described by Herbert Feis, Economic Advisor to the Department of State from 1931 to 1937 and Advisor on International Economic Affairs until 1943. Professor Feis has subsequently been a member of the Institute for Advanced Study at Princeton and is the author of numerous books concerned with contemporary problems in international relations, among them *The Road to Pearl Harbor* (1950) and *Churchill — Roosevelt — Stalin* (1957).

DURING this whole period — in which Italian aggression was prepared and begun — Washington was an important station in the circuit of indecision. It is time to take account of what had been occurring there.

To the Italian dictator the American course was of the utmost importance. He seems to have felt assured that the mistrust pervading the relations between the states of Europe would prevent collective action to check him, unless some outside power bolstered the attempt. There was only one country strong enough and free enough to turn the balance of events against him, if it so willed — the United States.

The peoples of Europe prayed that the Americans would provide the supporting strength to defend them against the demanding threats that issued from Rome and Berlin. Over all the roads of Europe apparitions appeared at dawn and night — of dirty, haggard men in muddy uniforms limping towards the trenches, of exhausted and frightened women and children trudg-

ing out of destroyed towns. To the imaginative, the throats of Mussolini and Hitler poured forth not human words, but mud and lice and pieces of bloody flesh.

The governments of Europe did not give way to such fantasies or tremors. But as they probed to see how much they could rely on one another in any joint effort to check Mussolini, they peered in the direction of the United States. They knew the state of American opinion well enough to realize that the United States would not keep in regular step with them. They accepted the evidence that the American people were bent upon believing that European quarrels were of little concern to them and beyond their power to reconcile. They responded to intimations that if openly asked to act with the League, the American government would look the other way. But as soon as the League began to consider ways and means of halting Italian aggression, two most practical questions arose in regard to American policy: First, if economic sanctions were applied, would the

United States render them futile by supplying economic aid to Italy? Second, if as an outcome of the use of sanctions, Italy attacked members of the League, would the United States be an indifferent and difficult neutral, a benevolent friend, or an ally?

The League members were left to the end to guess the full answers to these questions. They were compelled by use of the telescope to discern what they could from obscure actions and smoky explanations.

During the summer months of 1935, when Italian intentions were becoming obvious, neither the American people nor the American government were moved to take any step that might seriously deter Mussolini. Many Americans sensed uneasily that deadly evil was being given a new passport into the world. But the country as a whole either misunderstood or evaded the coming crisis. We restricted ourselves to some half measures gauged, at one and the same time, to absolve us of any charge of defeating collective action and lessen the chance of being drawn into dispute with any belligerent. A wish to avoid responsibility, rather than any positive will to play a part in defeating aggression, governed our swaying policy.

The request, made in July by the Ethiopian government that we invoke the pact of Paris against Italy, had met only sympathetic evasion. The State Department, during the following week, pursued a conventional diplomatic course. In various ways it made plain to the Italian government that it was disturbed by the dangerous drift of events. It dwelt upon the rewards and virtues of peace and urged Italy to be moderate. But at the same time it discreetly took care to see that the foreign offices of Great Britain and France did not misinterpret these *démarches*. Ways were found to make sure that they were not to be taken as a promise that we would take positive action or an encouragement for a new attempt to draw us into joint responsibility.

While the failure of the League at medi-ation was becoming plain, the President on July 24 responded to intensely active agitation throughout the country. He asked Congress to consider "neutrality" legislation. A few days thereafter (July 26), he lapsed into the remark that the Italo-Ethiopian dispute was not of direct concern to the United States. On August 1, he expressed the hope that the Council of the League would succeed in settling the issues that had arisen. This wish could have been met as well by a settlement that gave in to Italy as by a firm refusal to do so. These actions were expressions of a transient half belief that the United States might wisely pursue an isolated course — no matter who gained power and mastery elsewhere.

But they also suited a purpose. That was to keep control of the making of foreign policy in the face of an effort, within Congress and outside, to impose upon the Executive rigid rules of isolation, amounting almost to nonintercourse. It was feared that any overt measure of encouragement to the League to repress Italy would strengthen the position of the advocates of isolation.

It was deemed certain that any action that aligned the United States with the League, even before it was known whether Great Britain and France would defend the principles of the League, would provoke a bitter internal conflict. In their earlier days, many of the officials that were now compelled to decide how to act in this crisis of aggression had witnessed closely the failure and death of Woodrow Wilson. The popular mood seemed far more averse to any venture in co-operation than in 1919. They were afraid of repeating his failure.

Several groups in Congress vied with each other in order to secure the credit for the new policy of peace. The Senate Committee on Foreign Relations, the House Committee on Foreign Affairs, and the group of extreme isolationists led by Nye and Clarke, each sprang forward with a program designed to keep us clear of foreign strife. All refused to admit that the American people had an earnest concern with any foreign dispute, or a possible great interest in its outcome. It was as though they thought there could be no rights or wrongs of consequence to us outside the Western Hemisphere, no purpose ever in taking up arms, no hope of trustful cooperation between nations.

The Senators in their visits to the White House met no opposition to their plans for the enactment of some new form of neutrality legislation. The Secretary of State and some of his staff smouldered with doubt in regard to what was underway. But this was permitted to appear only as a faint glow. The Senate combinations seemed strong enough to defeat any Secretary of State on this question, and, if his opposition was vigorous, to destroy him. Therefore, such powers of persuasion as he possessed were gently employed towards trying to obtain in the prospective legislation some discretion for the Executive. But that is exactly what the extreme and powerful isolationist and anti-British wing of the Senate was determined to deny.

Congress passed and the President signed the Neutrality Resolution in August 1935 while the League was permitting Italy to complete its military measures. The timing of our action was influenced by discernment that Italy was about to break the world's peace; and that the League would either have to knuckle down or to fight. In either event, embarrassing difficulties were foreseen — which, it was thought, might be "shooed" away by *prior* proclamation of our isolation.

Despite the enthusiastic furor with which the Neutrality Resolution was rushed through Congress, a sense remained in many minds that the subject had not been thoroughly considered. Therefore, it was made effective only until February 20, 1936. This temporary legislation was counted upon by its advocates to guarantee the good behavior of the President during the prospective recess of Congress.

The Neutrality Resolution made it mandatory upon the President, on finding that a state of war existed, to prohibit the sale or export of "arms, ammunition, and implements of war" to all belligerents. Americans were left free to trade in all other products — including many no less essential for war. The dividing line was arbitrary. It reflected the fact that not even the isolationist Senators were ready to push their theory of peace to the point where it might seriously disturb American economic life.

The actual substance of the Neutrality Resolution had little immediate importance. Its passage, nevertheless, had great significance. For it seemed to reveal what the American attitude would be toward the critical issues that were shaping up in the Italo-Ethiopian dispute. It seemed to mean, first, that if foreign countries found themselves at war — whether in support of their obligations as members of the League or in self-defense — they could not count upon the United States to supply weapons. And second, if they refused, as a sanction, to trade with the aggressor, it was doubtful whether the United States would do the same. In that case, the whole idea of economic sanctions grew hollow; only blockade could prevail, and that meant war.

True, this was a hasty interpretation of the ultimate significance of the passage of the resolution; palmistry, rather than penetration. But only those with deep insight into the intelligence and moral nature of the American people could have been expected to dispute it. Ironically this interpretation was longer maintained in Berlin than in London; it contributed to fatal German misjudgment of the ultimate American course.

The passage of the Neutrality Resolution dampened the spirit of resistance to Mussolini. As reported by Birchell in the *New York Times* of August 26, the resolution "disappointed and even discouraged many here (London) who had hoped for United States cooperation in compelling the truculent to keep the peace. Coming during a period when the League members were wavering between their conciliation efforts and proposals to apply collective punitive action to Italy, it must have justified doubt in those circles of European government, as to the wisdom or significance of such punitive action."

But it is also certain that the action of the American government was not the main reason for the hesitation of the League. Almost none of its members were ready to fight Italy.

A strong element in British opinion clamored for collective action. But many of its public advocates seemed to infer that this form of action was a sort of magical prescription that would safely and painlessly dispose of any evil-doer. They seemed to think that condemnatory words, if hurled in unison, would halt dictators. Few spokesmen asked their fellow countrymen bluntly if they were willing, if need should be, to go to war against the Blackshirts. And the British military establishment, even its navy, was unready for immediate action. Nervousness seems to have entered even into the paneled rooms of the admiralty. The mementos of past valor and victories did not entirely dissipate fear that the Italian fleet might be able to gain control over the eastern Mediterranean and the direct route to India. Or if that fear was dismissed, the thought was left that a damaged fleet might someday soon have to deal with a stronger enemy. In the Foreign Office there was a great reluctance to smash the Stresa front, which had been formed against Germany by such hard diplomatic labors. The hope lingered that Italy might be retained as a useful ally.

And France was resisting all suggestion of pressure on Italy with a firmness that aroused mistrust, as well it might. The government of Laval showed itself determined to avoid any quarrel with Italy that would rupture their relations. He was prepared, if need be, to sacrifice the League in favor of his understanding with Mussolini. French opinion was wavering and divided. There were many — especially among the Left parties — who were devoted believers in the cause of the League, friends of all that was humane, and enemies of all that was cruel. But they were mostly men skilled only in the argument and appeal of the classroom or political meetings; they had not yet lived in the maquis and been toughened to the use of arms; and they did not control French opinion or their government. Fear of Germany reconciled many Frenchmen to Laval's open effort to serve Mussolini; fear of Russia brought approval from many others; fear of again experiencing the dreadful sorrow and suffering of war, most of all. Laval could warn that there would be civil war in France if that country was called upon to fight Italy. His opponents could not threaten that there would be civil war if the League bowed before Fascism.

This was the main gambit of doubt and deception that kept England wavering and France evasive. It was why they and the other countries of Europe failed to form a quick and effective combination in the League to halt Italy. However, each item of doubt gained extra weight because of the judgment that the United States would either stand aside, or even make such an attempt more difficult and dangerous. The passage of the Neutrality Resolution confirmed that possibility.

In the interval between the passage of the Neutrality Resolution and the Italian invasion of Ethiopia, American policy continued to be as elusive as notes dancing in air. The Italian proclamations of defiance were becoming noisier and noisier. Reports on the tangled talks between the British and French governments produced complete uncertainty in Washington as to what to expect at Geneva. The American government supplemented the confusion of counsel in Europe by diffuse and inconclusive explanations of its own. The Secretary of State on September 12 circulated a detailed account of the record of the American government, vis-à-vis the Italian-Ethiopian dispute. This was intended both as a defense for our policy and an indirect means of renewing our plea that peace should not be broken. Its long explanations left only a sense of emptiness. It did not affect the course of events in any way. Nor did the repetition of the plea for peace which was made by the President on the following day.

The vague utterances were disregarded. The American multigraph machine failed. Hoping it knew not what, the American government waited for the next event. It waited uneasily. For the perception that only collective actions could really safeguard future peace for the United States, though dismissed, would not quit the mind. A vague realization that the outcome of the League crisis would affect our future would not fade.

Alas, when the wait was ended by the Italian invasion of Ethiopia on October 3, it was succeeded only by a greater agony of indecision.

We had missed any chance decisively to influence events before the crisis. We had remained aloof while they shaped into an Italian threat not only against Ethiopia but against the whole League system. Then on the very eve of the clash we merely issued a statement urging all countries to support economic and world peace. Its inchoate stream of language seemed to suggest that the ultimate causes of the episode were economic and that if only trade barriers were removed, the aggressive pressure for political change would vanish. It was as though we thought that by holding up high the scales of abstract justice disputants would come into court and bring their sins with them. Circumstances of the moment did not justify the thought.

Now events began to compel the government to move from the court of comment to the field of decision. Of the many aspects of the problem before the American government only one was clear. It was agreed by all that the President was bound to recognize that war had come and apply the Neutrality Resolution. But the problem arose as to when to do so. Italy had issued no declaration of war; that country was still hoping that the world would shut its ears to the noise of exploding bombs. The League of Nations was in a state of pause. Should the American government be the first to affirm that war existed? There was room for query as to what immediate consequences might flow from that formal action. Would it make it more difficult for Italy to draw back? Would it embarrass last-minute efforts of the League to halt the fighting by conciliation?

Behind these perplexities lay further ones. If the government applied the Neutrality Resolution and did nothing more, how might the later conduct of Italy and the League be affected? Would this step be taken to mean that we intended otherwise to ignore the Italian aggression, to give up all thought of dealing with it? Would this be a true reading of what the country might later decide to do? The executive was in no position to encourage hope that we would help effectively in any joint effort to stop Italy, but most Americans were ready to applaud the efforts of other countries to do so. Would an unsupplemented announcement of American neutrality give reluctant members of the League an acceptable reason for inaction? Would it enable them to place the blame for failure of the League upon the United States?

The government craved a course of action that would be without consequence on external events. It wished for a line that could neither be attacked as calculated encouragement to the League to proceed with sanctions against Italy, nor used by unwilling members of the League as an excuse for not doing so. The lawyers of the State Department labored to supply a garment of formulas within which we could shrink.

Their task was made more difficult by the knowledge that Congress would insist that we deal with *all* belligerents on the same terms. Suppose the executive action went outside the Neutrality Resolution and tried, for example, to repress the flow of American war materials to Italy. Would it find itself driven to deny them also to England and France, if these countries found themselves at war with Italy?

The meetings of disturbed officials during the days that followed the invasion of Ethiopia were a convention hall of these queries. Every single one of them paraded around under its own banner. The President was away from Washington. Views had to be discussed over the telephone and telegraph when he could be reached.

On the one point that was clear, decision was prompt. The President and the Secretary of State concluded to recognize that war existed without waiting for the League to do so, and to place the mandatory provisions of the Neutrality Resolution into effect. It was their plain duty under the law so to act. The possibility that this precedent might later be regretted would have to be disregarded. Immediate application of the resolution had still another attraction to minds caught in a multiple spray of cold doubt; it would serve as a proof of the contention that had been carefully maintained by the State Department that American action was independent of that of other nations.

This decision was made in the face of an urgent plea of the American Minister at Geneva to delay. He was opposed to an American declaration that war existed before the Council of the League affirmed it. He feared the stain of responsibility on our cuff if we moved our hand first.

During the days of October 4 and 5, when the proclamations were being prepared, forecasts in Washington of what the Council might decide to do were scant and confused. The British government was in the direct line of conflict. Thus, when the proclamations were ready, it was thought a reasonable precaution and courtesy to afford it a chance to object to their immediate issuance. No objection was made.

The President proceeded to declare that "a state of war unhappily exists between Ethiopia and the Kingdom of Italy." One proclamation was issued prohibiting shipment of arms, ammunition, and implements of war to the belligerents. Another requested American citizens not to travel on the ships of belligerents and stated that if they did so it was at their own risk.

In announcing this action, and in all later expositions of our course throughout the episode, the State Department emphasized that they were taken in entire independence of other countries. Any suggestion that heed was being taken of events at Geneva was indignantly denied; any contention that it was our duty to prevent Italian aggression was answered with silence. The country was repeatedly informed that the government had but one thought or aim — to "keep out of war."

This explanation of the basis of our policy was irritating to all except those American officials who were in the center of the buffeting storm. It was immune from direct objection. It conformed to the prevailing American opinion that joint action with other countries would "involve" us in war. It made it possible to avoid a debate that would almost certainly have been lost; whether or not the security and welfare of the United States demanded a concert of action with foreign powers.

Here in this Ethiopian dispute were born the verbal formulas that were used to explain and defend many important actions of the Executive during the troubled years ahead — first, that they were independently conceived and taken, and second, that they were designed solely to keep the United States out of war. By their use it was possible for American diplomacy to achieve a measure of freedom from the restraints of ignorance and lethargy. But they failed ever to direct the full force of American influence or power to prevent developments that made war inevitable. Friends were left without assurance. Foes could form the belief that the American instinct for greatness, hatred of evil, and shrewdness had lapsed. But the bitter unwillingness of American opinion to mingle in foreign disputes exacted from their leaders this insufficient and misleading version of the realities they had to take into account. . . .

THE MYTH OF COLLECTIVE PACIFISM

RICHARD H. S. CROSSMAN

Richard H. S. Crossman, politician and journalist, Labour member of parliament since 1945, was also assistant editor of the *New Statesman and Nation* from 1943 to 1955. Author of numerous penetrating studies of the role of socialism in the world today, he also edited the moving collection of essays by disillusioned former Communists entitled *The God That Failed* (1950). In the selection below from *Government and the Governed* published in 1939, Mr. Crossman tries to analyze the essential meaning of collective security in the inter-war years.

THE post-war epoch is only intelligible when we grasp the moral and spiritual conservatism of the Peace settlement. The attempt to extend democratic principles beyond the shifting confines of the nation state was not made. Instead, the old order of nation states was re-established, the colonial empires enlarged, economic imperialism encouraged and central Europe balkanized. Such a settlement would have been excusable on one condition, that it was recognized for what it was, a temporary expedient hurriedly thrown together by exhausted politicians. But this did not happen. On the contrary, the peace was ushered in with a blowing of moral trumpets unprecedented in history. Wilson, anxious to save his face, argued that the settlement was in accordance with his Fourteen Points, and the peoples of the victor nations were taught to believe that a new era of international order had begun. An old-fashioned treaty was decked out with all the attributes of a new dispensation, and the German nation was denounced as guilty of the world war.

The result was that the peoples of the victorious democracies were lulled into an easy acquiescence. Believing (for men will always believe what they want to believe) that peace and justice had been established, they assumed that no more needed to be done. First the Covenant of the League and disarmament, and then Collective Security, became for the common man the symbols of international righteousness, and a strange new philosophy spread, particularly in England. "Collective Pacifism" sufficiently describes its character.

This theory held that power politics had in fact been abolished and that, since the rule of International Law was an accomplished fact, the peoples of the world could rely upon the Covenant of the League for their security. Now that the civilized nations were united in their abhorrence of aggression, world-wide responsibilities could lightly be undertaken simultaneously with an extensive disarmament. The unpleasant fact that Collective Security might mean British war was discreetly veiled under the name of sanctions, just as the extension of the colonial empires had been disguised as mandates.

The myth of collective security captured the progressive Liberals of England just as the myth of the U.S.S.R. captured the Socialist Left. What actually happened in

From *Government and the Governed* by R. H. S. Crossman (New York, 1939), pp. 253–258. Published by G. P. Putnam's Sons. In Great Britain by Christophers, Ltd. Used by permission of the publishers.

Russia or Geneva was immaterial to people who desired less to organize peace and justice than to believe that peace and justice were already organized. The trained Marxist and the intelligent Conservative, who ridiculed these airy visions, were regarded as brutal materialists by people whose ignorance of foreign affairs was only matched by their desire for a secular religion to replace the orthodox Christianity which they had mostly lost. Russia and the League became articles of belief for growing sections of public opinion which were able to unite when Russia joined the League in 1934.

This was the first occasion on which the Left in Great Britain had evolved its own foreign policy. Previous to 1914 such matters had remained outside the sphere of party politics because the balance of power had been for so long an undisputed dogma. It is not surprising therefore, that the British Left accepted President Wilson as its prophet and brushed aside all doubts of the new dispensation. Anti-militarism and anti-imperialism had been for generations strong in all classes and had gained added strength since the Boer War. To these negative feelings were now added a positive creed, which satisfied the consciences of democrats who had been vaguely worried by British imperialism.

We have observed previously that political ideas percolate upwards, and that the British middle classes constantly impress their ideology upon the rulers of the country. The post-war period was no exception to this rule. Great Britain was crippled by debts, and soon discovered that she would be unable easily to regain her pre-war trade. Though in the early years the Conservatives preferred isolation and permitted the French to rule Europe, they soon discovered that economic recovery was impossible without a revival of Germany and a restoration of European confidence. This was achieved at Locarno in 1925, and from that year onwards Conservative opinion became gradually converted to League ideals. Since there was no potential ag-

gressor, it seemed easy to accept the Covenant and to relieve taxation by easing the armament programme. Without any immediate sacrifice of imperial interests, Britain was able to accept the League idea.

Seen in retrospect, the period from 1918–1933 is marked by a growing lethargy in the victor nations. Neither at home nor abroad did democracy undertake a single great constructive enterprise. Victory seemed to have deprived France and Britain of their dynamic: their Conservatives ceased to be ardent imperialists, and their Socialists lost their revolutionary fervour. A spirit of collective pacifism possessed them, and made the peoples content with the lazy approval of high ideals, the verbal condemnation of injustice, chicanery and oppression. Holding all the power, the Western democracies disdained to use it, so long as the status quo was in any way tolerable. The attitude of America was not dissimilar, except that here the League idea was rejected and the Monroe doctrine was still regarded as America's contribution to world peace.

A myth is only justifiable if it stimulates to action. But "Collective Pacifism" was a sedative, not a stimulant. It intoxicated the democracies with a feeling of moral superiority and well-being, while it sapped their sense of responsibility. Gradually statesmen and peoples alike began to believe that the League of Nations was a force able to do the work which previously fell to the various nations. Instead of relying on themselves and on co-operation with their allies, they began to rely on the League to preserve peace. Since the League had no coercive power at its disposal, this trust was wholly unjustified.

No one Party or section of the population can be blamed for this collapse of democratic morale. The great opportunity had been missed in 1918–19: and it was difficult for the Western democracies to recover from that failure. They had encouraged nationalism as the basis of government; they had retained economic imperialism and permitted international finance to function independently of government policy. In brief, they had as far as possible returned to pre-war conditions. Having done so, they sought to humanize them. That they failed is an indication that good intentions and kindness, unbacked by resolution and knowledge, may disguise injustices but never eradicate them. Kindness and good-will no doubt console the patient suffering from cancer, but they will not cure the cancer; and the patient whose practitioner only displays these qualities, may, in his intolerable agonies, turn to a quack and curse the Christian humanity which his practitioner displays.

The growth of Fascism is only intelligible against the background of Collective Pacifism. Though in each case its immediate cause was internal economic distress, both its philosophy and its success are largely due to the international situation produced by the Anglo-French hegemony of the post-war years. Since the Western democracies had so lamentably failed to organize the world for peace, the Fascists have been able without much difficulty to organize it for war. Since France and England were determined at all costs to retain the sovereignty of the nation state, Fascism has mobilized the nation against the League Powers. Since the democratic victors refused to recognize racial equality, Fascism has made racial inequality into a principle of policy. Against democracies too lethargic to end the exploitation of colonial peoples, Fascism has begun a new crusade which openly glorifies imperialism as a national right of the nobler races. In brief, it has selected from Liberal democracy all its nationalism and imperialism, stripped them of their humanitarianism and displayed them to the world in all their nakedness.

SUGGESTIONS FOR ADDITIONAL READING

The student interested in gaining a fuller understanding of the part played by the Ethiopian Crisis as a crucial steppingstone on the path which led to the Second World War should first turn to a general survey of the international situation in the interwar years. In detail there is nothing to surpass Arnold J. Toynbee, ed., *Survey of International Affairs 1920–1939* (London, 1925–40). Volume II of the Survey for 1935 is devoted completely to Italy and Ethiopia. See also another publication of the Royal Institute of International Affairs, *International Sanctions* (London, 1938). Both G. M. Gathorne-Hardy, *A Short History of International Affairs 1920–1939* (London, 1950), 4th ed., a selection from which is included in this booklet, and E. H. Carr, *International Relations Between the Two World Wars 1929–1939* (London, 1947), present a critical review of these years. A more trenchant account is Frederick L. Schuman, *Europe on the Eve* (New York, 1939). L. B. Namier, *Europe in Decay: A Study in Disintegration, 1936–1940* (London, 1950), has written a finely perceptive study of a more limited span of years. Hajo Holborn, *The Political Collapse of Europe* (New York, 1951), provides perhaps the best broad framework within which the catastrophe can be perceived.

A great deal was written on the Ethiopian Crisis in 1935 and the years immediately following. The quality of this material is mixed, and most of it is not cited here, but *The Abyssinian Dispute, the Background of the Conflict* (by a group of expert students of international affairs, Carnegie Endowment for International Peace, New York, 1935) provides an immediate background. The war itself is covered by Walter Millis, *Why Europe Fights* (New York, 1940), and Herbert Matthews, *Eyewitness in Abyssinia* (New York, 1938). A. H. Jones and Elizabeth Monroe, *A History of Ethiopia* (London, 1935), can be supplemented by Elizabeth MacCallum, *Rivalries in Ethiopia* (Boston, 1935), and Ernest Work, *Ethiopia, a Pawn in European Diplomacy* (New York, 1935); Daniel Haskell, *Ethiopia and the Italo-Ethiopian Conflict 1928–1936: A Selected List of References* (New York, 1936), and Helen F. Conover, *Ethiopia: A Selective List of Recent Works* (Washington, 1947).

The position played by the League is incisively outlined by Sir Alfred Zimmern, *The League of Nations and the Rule of Law* (London, 1939), 2nd ed.; also F. P. Walters' detailed *A History of the League of Nations* (London, 1952), 2 vol. Vera Micheles Dean makes an optimistic survey in "The League and the Italo-Ethiopian Crisis" in *Foreign Policy Reports* (New York, 1935), vol. xi, no. 18. See also Albert Highley, *The First Sanction Experiment: A Study in League Procedures* (Geneva, 1938); Pitman B. Potter, *The Wal Wal Arbitration* (Washington, 1938); André Mandelstam, *Le conflit italo-éthiopien devant la Société des Nations* (Paris, 1937).

The best accounts of Italian policy in English are the antithetical works of Gaetano Salvemini, *Prelude to World War II* (New York, 1954), and Luigi Villari, *Italian Foreign Policy Under Mussolini* (New York, 1956). But see also Maxwell Macartney and Paul Cremona, *Italy's Foreign and Colonial Policy 1914–1937* (London, 1938), and René Albrecht-Carrié, *Italy from Napoleon to Mussolini* (New York, 1950). Benedetto Croce, *L'Europa e l'Italia* (Bari, 1944), and Carlo Sforza's short study, *France et Italie: demain, il faut faire grand* (Rome, 1944), present the liberal Italian point of view. Emilio de Bono, *Anno XIII — The Conquest of an Empire* (London, 1937) describes the Italian preparations for war.

Alexander Werth, *The Twilight of France, 1933–1940* (New York, 1942); Dennis W. Brogan, *The Development of*

Modern France (1870–1939) (London, 1944), and *The French Nation: From Napoleon to Pétain* (London, 1957); and René Albrecht-Carrié, *France, Europe and the Two World Wars* (New York, 1961), analyze the involved political position of France in the 1930's. Charles A. Micaud, *The French Right and Nazi Germany, 1933–1939* (Durham, 1943), is an excellent study of French public opinion. Pierre Laval has been the subject of much speculation: David Thomson, *Two Frenchmen: Pierre Laval and Charles de Gaulle* (London, 1951); Alfred Mallet, *Pierre Laval* (Paris, 1955), 2 vol., are the most objective. See also Henry Torrès, *Pierre Laval* (London, 1941); Pierre Tissier, *I Worked with Laval* (London, 1942); Pierre Laval, *The Diary of Pierre Laval* (New York, 1948), for more controversial evidence. Laval's successor presents his case in Pierre-Etienne Flandin, *Politique française, 1919–1940* (Paris, 1947). André Géraud (Pertinax), *The Gravediggers of France: Gamelin, Daladier, Reynaud, Pétain and Laval* (New York, 1944), and Geneviève Tabouis, *They Called Me Cassandra* (New York, 1942), were influential journalists of the time. André François-Poncet, *The Fateful Years: Memoirs of a French Ambassador in Berlin, 1931–1938* (New York, 1949) views the crisis from the vantage point of an influential diplomat.

D. C. Somervell, *British Politics since 1900* (London, 1950), provides a spirited survey of this subject. Chapter XIX of Arnold Wolfers, *Britain and France between Two Wars* (New York, 1940), dissects British-Italian relations as cleanly as does the selection on France and Italy in this booklet. This is also true of W. M. Jordan, *Great Britain, France and the German Problem: A Study of Anglo-French Relations in the Making and Maintenance of the Versailles Settlement* (London, 1944). In addition to Winston Churchill, *The Gathering Storm* (Cambridge, Mass., 1948), the views of the English statesman appear clearly in Richard H. Powers, "Winston Churchill's Parliamentary Commentary on British Foreign Policy, 1935–1938," *Journal of Modern History*, XXVI (June, 1954). Concerning other British political figures, see G. M. Young, *Stanley Baldwin* (London, 1952); Lewis Broad, *Anthony Eden: The Chronicle of a Career* (New York, 1955); Lord Robert Vansittart, *Lessons of My Life* (New York, 1943); Sir Samuel Hoare, Viscount Templewood, *Nine Troubled Years* (London, 1954). The implications of British policy are treated in Ernst Preisseisen, "Foreign Policy and British Public Opinion: The Hoare-Laval Pact of 1935," *World Affairs Quarterly* (October, 1958). Speeches by both Hoare and Laval are found in *Vital Speeches of the Day*, Vols. I and II, October 1934–October 1936 (London, 1935, 1936). William L. Langer, "The Struggle for the Nile," *Foreign Affairs*, XIV (January, 1936), takes note of British imperial considerations.

Germany, which benefited to such an extent from the crisis, was not an active participant. Good accounts are Alan Bullock, *Hitler: A Study in Tyranny* (New York, 1952); Elizabeth Wiskemann, *The Rome-Berlin Axis: A History of the Relations Between Hitler and Mussolini* (Oxford, 1949); Paul Seabury, *The Wilhelmstrasse: A Study of German Diplomats Under the Nazi Regime* (Berkeley, 1954); William A. Shirer, *The Rise and Fall of the Third Reich* (New York, 1960). Foreign policy in general is the concern of Gordon A. Craig and Felix Gilbert (eds.), *The Diplomats, 1919–1939* (Princeton, 1953). For that of Russia, see Max Beloff, *The Foreign Policy of Soviet Russia 1929–1941* (London, 1947), 2 vols.

Edwin Borchard and William P. Lage, *Neutrality for the United States* (New Haven, 1940), 2nd ed.; Charles C. Tansill, *Back Door to War: The Roosevelt Foreign Policy 1933–1941* (Chicago, 1952); Charles A. Beard, *American Foreign Policy in the Making, 1932–1940: A Study in Responsibilities* (New Haven, 1946), present the case for American isolationism. This is countered by Selig Adler, *The Isolationist*

Impulse: Its Twentieth-Century Reaction (New York, 1957), and Herbert Feis, *Seen from E. A.: Three International Episodes* (New York, 1947) who analyzes the search for national security in narrating the attempt in the 1930's to secure adequate supplies of rubber and oil. See also H. Stuart Hughes, *The United States and Italy* (Oxford, 1954); John Norman, "Influence of Pro-Fascist Propaganda on American Neutrality, 1935–1936," in *Essays in History and International Relations: In Honor of George Hubbard Blakeslee* (Dwight Lee and George McReynolds, eds., Worcester, Mass., 1949); and Ursula Hubbard, "The Cooperation of the United States with the League of Nations, 1931–1936" in *International Conciliation*, No. 329, Carnegie Endowment for International Peace (New York, 1937).

The background of the famous Peace Ballot is described by Dame Adelaide Livingstone, *The Peace Ballot: The Official History* (London, 1935), and Lord Robert Cecil, *A Great Experiment* (Oxford, 1941). A study of public opinion is provided in Helen Hiett, *Public Opinion and the Italo-Ethiopian Dispute* (Geneva, 1936), and P. Vaucher and P. H. Siriex, *L'opinion britannique, la Société des Nations et la guerre italo-éthiopienne* (Paris, 1936). Of particular interest are the contemporary issues of *The Nation* (New York) and *The New Republic* (New York) in whose columns the confusions of the pre-war years are graphically reflected.